GREEN RETAIL DESIGN

GREEN RETAIL DESIGN

MARTIN M. PEGLER

ST MEDIA
GROUP
INTERNATIONAL

Cincinnati, Ohio

ISBN 10: 0-944094-68-6
ISBN 13: 978-0-944094-68-6

Published by:

ST Books — a division of
ST Media Group International Inc.
11262 Cornell Park Drive
Cincinnati, Ohio 45242
U.S.A.

Phone 513-263-9399
Fax 513-744-6999
Email: books@stmediagroup.com
Internet: www.bookstore.stmediagroup.com

Distributed outside the U.S. to the book and art trade by:

Collins Design, an Imprint of HarperCollinsPublishers
10 East 53rd Street
New York, NY 10022
www.harperdesigninternational.com

Cover and book design by Kim Pegram, Senior Art Director, *VMSD* and *Hospitality Style*
Book proofread by Matt Hall, Online Editor, *VMSD* and *Hospitality Style*
Proofreading assisted by Tyler Grote

Printed in China

10 9 8 7 6 5 4 3 2 1

Acknowledgements

This book and many of my others would not have been possible without the help and cooperation of the numerous architects, designers and visual merchandisers around the world who provided me with the high resolution images of their new and unique projects. I am able to report on what is happening in store design and display only through their generosity.

When I started to write this book, I sent out hundreds of emails to the many talented people I have worked with over the years. Through their submissions, or following up on their suggestions to contact people they knew, this book took form. I want to thank all those whose projects appear in this book and the many others who did not have green projects to offer, but had ideas or thoughts that they shared with me. Thanks to them for their advice and assistance. I also greatly appreciate the cooperative spirit of the photographers who graciously allowed us to reproduce their artwork.

Thank you to Ashley Katz, the Communications Manager at the USGBC for her help, her information, her permission for us to reprint the LEED checklist at the back of the book, and for her contribution to the first section of the book. Thanks also to Ted Ning, Executive Director of LOHAS, for his introductory remarks. I was pleased to reprint excerpts from writings by Prof. Hallier, the Managing Director of the EHI Retail Institute and President of the European Retail Academy; and Helmut Neher, the Executive Director of the Umdasch Shopfittng Group. David Wright, of Dalziel+Pow Design Consultancy of London, was most kind to share his thoughts on greening and the plight of the designer in the greening process. To all the above, I truly am indebted for the material and the education I received.

A special thanks goes to my friend, Wolfgang Gruschwitz who—in a way—was the "father" of this book. It was while listening to him speaking about Sustainability at an International Housewares Association conference in Chicago that I wrote down "Reuse, Repurpose, Recycle" as the words appeared in his PowerPoint presentation. Looking back at those words, a few weeks later, this book actually began.

My "son", Jess Resnick, is probably the only person who has ever really read any of my books and he has done it willingly and without being prodded. This time he graciously took on the onerous task of proofing the copy and for that-- and many other things—a very big "thanks."

Way back in 1970 ST Media Group (then known as Signs of the Times Publishing Co.) published my second and third books, Show & Sell and Tell & Sell. Now, forty years later I am delighted that they are publishing my seventy-seventh book and I'm looking forward to a few more. "Thank you," Mark Kissling, for all of your efforts on my behalf.

A great big "thanks" to the Retail Design Industry for giving me a home and a place where I find things of interest and can do things that make me interesting.

And lastly, a "thank you" that is long overdue—to Suzan, who always stands besides me (or a little behind me), makes me look good and pushes me forward while still keeping me in check. This "thank you" comes with all my love.

Martin M. Pegler

CONTENTS

Introduction

Whether it is your regular daily newspaper, a fashion magazine, a trade publication, an intellectual paper on economics or a "save the whales" brochure in the mail—there is no way you can escape the tsunami that is Greening/Sustainability. These two words—irritant or inspiration—will not go away. The Gospel of Greening is spreading and along with it we have "eco-friendly," "energy efficient," "recyclable,"

"reuse" and "repurpose." With our growing concern for the world we know and the world our children and our children's children will inherit, enlightened architects/designers and store planners around the world are learning more about ecology and applying new concepts, practices and materials to their design solutions. Also, more and more retailers and international brands are showing their concern for the earth and its future and are demanding greener, more eco-friendly retail settings in which to showcase their products or introduce and promote their services. Readers will note that numerous projects in this book are Green because it was one of the design objectives set forth by the retailer.

Currently, in the U.S., the main arbiter of Greening is LEED (Leadership in Energy and Environmental Design). It has a commercial interior pilot program developed by the U.S. Green Building Council (USGBC) and it was specifically created for retailers. LEED has a rating system and awards certification based on that system that "addresses the unique nature of the retail environment and the different types of spaces that retailers need for their specific product lines." The scores are based on the LEED Green Building Rating System that is, according to USBGC, "a consensus-based national standard for developing environmentally responsible buildings." However, not all of the U.S. projects that have been included in this book are LEED certified. Not all retailers have as yet adopted the ecologically aware program for their brands. And yet, architects and designers are aware of the need for a Greener world. Wherever and whenever possible they are making an effort to incorporate sustainable and recyclable materials in their designs, and to adhere to the LEED recommendations.

There are many tints and shade of "Green" and though Greening is international, many countries do not have a system like LEED in place. Canada has adopted certification plan similar to LEED. Architects and designers in Europe, Asia, and South America are finding ways to design eco-friendly retail settings within the palette of Green, and so we have included examples of their work as well. Most have worked diligently on cutting the excess uses of energy, installed more efficient, low-heat lighting systems, reused existing materials or repurposed them to suit new situations. Though not as stringent as the LEED certification requirements, these architects and designers are overcoming, in many situations, the retailers' mistaken ideas about how much more expensive it is to "go Green." As one London designer put it in an interoffice paper, "We are the interface between clients and suppliers; we look at new materials, finishes and processes and can take the lead in investigating and investing in more sustainable ideas. We are committed to working together with our clients and our supply chains to deliver environmentally responsible design solutions, tackle issues at the creative stage and develop strategies for energy sustainability."

We admire, salute, congratulate and dedicate this book to the designers, architects and their clients whose products appear in this book. The dedication is also to my grandchildren: Brian, Amanda, Michael, Jacob, Samuel, Benjamin and Marley—and the millions of other grandchildren who can only benefit from these Green solutions.

Martin M. Pegler

A Statement From LEED
(Leadership in Energy and Environmental Design)

"As more consumers modify their lifestyle to become more eco-conscious, they are modifying their shopping preferences as well, to include not only what they buy but also where they shop. Eco-savvy customers are patronizing stores that embody their values—which means stores that are built and operated with green in mind. As a result, savvy retailers understand how buildings can add value to their brand. These retailers are turning to green building strategies and the LEED green building certification system to demonstrate and support their corporate social responsibility commitments, educate their customers and verify their accomplishments through third-party certification. Whether it's a specialty store or a big box retailer, the companies that go green are the companies that will make the most green.

Recognizing the unique nature of retail spaces, the U.S. Green Building Council (USGBC) has been working with the retail industry and a committee of industry experts to develop a certification system specifically for these types of projects. LEED for Retail New Construction and LEED for Retail Commercial Interiors, built on the experience of 96 pilot projects, is currently undergoing USGBC member ballot. Once the system passes ballot, it will provide certification paths for both ground-up retail construction and retail commercial interiors." — *Ashley Katz, Communications Manager, USGBC*

The U.S. Green Building Council's LEED green building certification system is the foremost program for the design, construction and operation of green buildings.35,000 projects are currently participating in the LEED system, comprising over 5.6 billion square feet of construction space in all 50 states and 114 countries.

By using less energy, LEED-certified buildings save money for families, businesses and taxpayers; reduce greenhouse gas emissions; and contribute to a healthier environment for residents, workers and the larger community.

USGBC was co-founded by current President and CEO Rick Fedrizzi, who spent 25 years as a Fortune 500 executive. Under his 15-year leadership, the organization has become the preeminent green buildingeducation and research organization in the nation.

For more information, visit www.usgbc.org.

BALENCIAGA

ANN DEMEULEMEESTER

Fashion + Fashion Accessories

Even haute couture can be green. Green is the color of fashion and the fashionable approach to retail design as viewed in the 91,500 sq.ft. building that houses Barneys New York store on the designer-filled Oak St. in Chicago. The smart and sophisticated interiors by Jeffrey Hutchison Associates of NY are ensconced in the LEED certified six-story luxury emporium created by the Gensler company's Chicago and New York offices. The new store, according to the Gensler teams,

has met "the official standards for environmentally sustainable construction in terms of efficiency, energy, atmosphere, materials and resources, indoor environmental quality, innovation and design process." In describing the new store, David New, Barneys New York executive VP of creative services, said, "We wanted the new store to resonate with the long history of great Chicago architecture, specifically the golden age of building that followed the Great Chicago Fire of 1871. In particular, the store pays tribute to the modern, classic approach of Louis Sullivan's building on State Street that is currently Carson Pirie Scott & Co."

As New said, Gensler's architects did reference the vocabulary of the late 19th century and the work of Sullivan. However, according

BARNEYS NEW YORK / FASHION + FASHION ACCESSORIES / **13**

to the Gensler teams, the unique architectural detail here is "the two monumental staircases," seen through the massive glass curtain wall that rise from the second level through to the fifth floor. From the limestone sheathed exterior, accented with bronze trim, the curved corner of the structure frames the staircases and shows them off to shoppers on Oak St. The spiraling staircases end in a stunning ceiling design patterned with blackened steel tracery. The numerous floor-to-ceiling windows in the new building are highlighted with scrims designed in collaboration with John Paul Philipe. The glazed openings allow daylight to flood onto each of the floors. Another green note is the use of outdoor terraces and "green" roofs filled with plantings. "The roof does not absorb heat. It reflects light, and returns oxygen to the atmosphere," New said.

The store interior features gallery-type settings in open floor plans. Each floor has its own unique design and character and the use of richer materials when compared to the old store—previously located across the street. The numerous intricate geometric floor patterns are executed in mosaic tiles, teak and end-cut timber as well as the glitzy organic stepping stone pattern in the Chelsea Passage department on the top floor. Shoppers enter into a ground floor with 14' ceilings—reminiscent of the "grand shopping emporiums of the early 20th century." Here, noted designer and brand name women's' fashion accessories and jewelry are located. To get down to the lower level where cosmetics and toiletries are set out on the white marble floor with its handsome geometric pattern, the shopper descends "down a geometric, sculptured staircase with sweeping vistas," according to Jeffrey Hutchison, the store's interior designer. This lower level is accentuated with backlit decorative murals "highlighting the product and conveying a clean, fresh sensibility."

Women's World is on the 2nd floor and it features a much enlarged Shoe Salon. The sample shoes "float" on the variegated acrylic shelving designed by the Jeffrey Hutchison Associates team. The balance of this floor is devoted to Women's Designer Apparel, which is defined by a contrasting gray limestone floor with a graphic triangular pattern. Bold light coves throughout the space "create a strong visual pattern," New said. Up on the 3rd floor is the CO-OP, which features a more industrial-inspired theme with oak, raw steel and whimsical painted furniture to create the desired look.

The rough hewn, end-grain wood floor on the 4th level identifies Men's Designer Clothing and Sportswear. The material and color palette includes oak, mahogany, white bronze and white lacquer—and the dark teak floors. The 5th floor—also for Menswear—has a more "clubby vibe" and has white wenge wood walls, bronze metal accents and teak floors. Chelsea Passage, the Barneys New York home shop, and Fred's, its signature eatery, share the light and airy 6th floor space.

In summing up his contributions to this store, Jeffrey Hutchison said, "Barneys has been at the forefront in incorporating a 'green' philosophy with fashion and with the Chicago project they were able to incorporate that philosophy with the architecture as well. It was important to evolve the store design to be environmentally sensitive while still achieving the Barneys mantra of Taste, Luxury and Humor."

This was accomplished in different ways. Natural daylight is a critical part of the store

design and an important environmental objective. This also allowed for more efficient lighting in the retail areas. Incorporating environmentally sensitive materials, such as cork and certified woods was important, as was having large portions of the millwork manufactured within a short distance from the site. Finally, construction practices such as using low VOC paints and adhesives, formaldehyde-free MDF and plywood in the cabinetry were effectively utilized.

This building reflects the taste and luxury of Chicago while staying true to the elegance that is synonymous with Barneys— and it's green.

Interior Design / Jeffrey Hutchison Associates, NY— Jeffrey Hutchison, Principal
Architectural Design / Gensler, NY & Chicago Studios—Chicago: Grant Uhlir, Principal in Charge (Core & Shell); Brian Vitale, Façade Design; Mark Spenser, Technical Director; Audrey Godwin, Project Architect
New York: Kathleen Jordan: Principal in Charge (Interiors); Katharine O'Toole, Project Manager; Na Kim, Job Captain
Photographer / Adrian Wilson

It's retro—it's Rock'n'Roll—and it's crammed full of reused, repurposed and recycled materials and props. It is the new/old John Varvatos Bowery NY store—the 10th Varvatos free-standing store—and it is comfortably situated in the Hard Rock Hotel & Casino in Las Vegas. The 3,000 sq.ft. space in many ways has the feel and groove of the original store in NYC's Bowery. The store is dark; it has the atmosphere of an underground music club from the '60s and '70s, and what is best of all is that the shop is filled with the award-winning designer's three collections; John Varvatos Collection, Star USA and Converse.

There can be no doubt that Varvatos looked to Rock'n'Roll's heritage for his inspiration. The space is filled with reclaimed memorabilia, vintage vinyl records and 1970s audio equipment. There is a stage with top of the line gear that includes a backline provided by Gibson Guitars, Marshall amplifiers, Yamaha drums and Zildjian cymbals. Complementing this performance area is a 30-ft. video wall that features iconic rock videos of all time and also serves as a background for live performances. The stage is used not only for staged events but also for impromptu jazz sessions from visiting rock stars and shoppers alike.

"Beyond my vision of fashion, I feel like we're bringing a unique bit of Rock'n'Roll culture to Las Vegas. It will also be a gathering place for both fans and artists," said John Varvatos.

Though the location is new, Varvatos—working in collaboration with the Meyer Davis Studio—has infused this location with the character and patina long associated with this brand. Aside from the vinyl records and period musical instruments and the sound equipment that add so much to the ambiance, there are the many reclaimed and repurposed elements. Varvatos found some of these items in the Paris flea markets that now show up here like the blackened steel doors, the gigantic factory fan that has been converted into a table top and the antique apothecary display that serves as the unique cash/wrap in the store. Then, there are the smokey mirrors, the chandelier and the industrial stage lighting—many reclaimed and rewired to serve in the shop's lighting design. Industrial metal mechanical parts have been repurposed to serve as display installations, side tables and fixtures. Thus, all the furnishings, furniture and fixtures are repurposed or found objects that add to the overall character of the space, and the suit area is set within an eclectic mix of old furniture reused

in a new way.

The store front showcases the reclaimed blackened steel doors and the reclaimed industrial hardware. Inside, the walls are sheathed in black brick and oxblood painted wood. Planks from the old Coney Island boardwalk are now used to sheath the walls. The reclaimed wood floors are accented with occasional planks of blackened steel stamped with the Varvatos "hallmark of authenticity"—a technique Varvatos discovered in a French factory. The overall effect is subtle—with a richly textured, rough hewn elegance, and a green solution in the reuse, repurpose, recycled and revived elements that not only create the space but give it its special aura.

Design Concept / John Varvatos
In collaboration with / Meyer Davis Studio, Inc.
Photography / Jeff Green

JOHN BARTLETT SHOP
Greenwich Village, NYC

There were very few changes that David Gauld, the architect / designer, could make to the store in the landmark building in Greenwich Village that now houses John Bartlett's wares. The relatively small space, only 500 sq.ft., is the flagship store for the up and coming, award-winning menswear designer. And yet, according to Gauld, "the storefront was rebuilt in a way that honors its historic style while also identifying its new use."

The design objective was to create, in this limited space, the essence of Bartlett's brand: sly, erotic, masculine and modern—delivered with a twist. The irregular shaped space has been given a focus by a central ceiling medallion and an overscaled light fixture. The ceiling was removed to expose the wood joists and also maximize the height in the shop. Because space is limited, the perimeter zone near the open ceiling is now used for storage. Glass and steel laboratory cabinets were installed over the hang rods and built-in

storage cabinets were added to the dressing room and toilet. Adding texture and interest, an original brick wall with exposed pipes was clad in dry stacked limestone "designed to enclose the pipes while creating niches to display merchandise," Gauld said. The tile that covered the pine sub-floor was removed and the original floor was pickled and now serves as the finished floor. Cabinets and wall panels were wrapped in linen and sealed with several coats of polyurethane. The material that was used for the "wrapping" was left over from Bartlett's previous season's line of clothing. The leather-covered countertop is also a reuse of previously used material.

In keeping with recycling, reusing and repurposing, the wall covering in the toilet is a decoupage of pages from vintage magazines and an eclectic but personal collection of items found at antique stores and thrift shops are used for display fixtures. Included in the recyclable materials category is the copper plumbing pipes and fittings that are cleverly combined and used as hanging racks. The poplar wood hangers are made from rapidly renewable material, and all the bags, tissue and gift boxes are made of recycled material and imprinted with eco-friendly inks. Since the stone veneer is thinly cut, it required only half the amount that would be necessary to cover the wall—and that also cut down the fuel costs in transporting the stone. The store is illuminated with low-voltage halogen lamps that are two times more efficient and last five times longer than incandescent lamps. They also save energy in the amount of power used for air-conditioning, since they produce much less heat.

In all, the new Bartlett shop suggests that a retail landmark has quietly been added to the storied Village scene.

Architecture & Design / David Gauld Architecture, NYC—David Gauld, Principal & Creative Director
Photography / Peter Dressel

I t is only a brief decade since 7 For All Mankind appeared on the retail scene with its collection of trend-setting , fashion-forward washes and designs in denim and jeans. Since then it has become a leader in the jeans market and created a true denim lifestyle brand that has become a favorite of Hollywood stars and other couture-consciouis, hip people.

The new retail store, located in an outdoor shopping center in Malibu, CA, was designed by 212 Design, Inc.—the design arm of InSite Development of NY, and according to the designers, "The store not only fits nicely into this beach community, but was also assembled with the environment in mind."

Greg Anderson, a principal at 212 Design said, "Since some of the best beaches and roadside surf shacks around are within walking dfistance to the boutique, the design had to be a natural evolution. Our focus was to maintain 7FAM's new expanding retail brand, capture the essence of Malibu—while still preserving the environment." Driftwood became the key element though "sourcing most other materials locally was the mission for creating a nonimpactful design."

The shop's design offers a low key, friendly, relaxed environment with the major emphasis on the presentation of the jeans. The all-white ambiance—walls, ceiling, floor and fixtures—is complemented by the natural reclaimed oak that is used to accentuate the wall fixtures. The fashion accessories are featured in the illuminated shadow box openings where energy-saving LED lighting is used. LED lights fill the ceiling as well to provide the store's overall illumination. The concrete floors and the white painted fixtures have been finished with low VOC (volatile organic compounds) paint to assure low levels of toxic emissions for years after application.

The focal rear wall is decoratively finished with reclaimed driftwood and behind it, screening off the dressing rooms, is a curtain made of a recycled organic cotton and hemp blend fabric. The occasional hassock seats are upholstered with a similar material. The changing rooms, behind the drape, are fitted with occupancy sensor lighting so that energy is conserved and used only as needed. Reclaimed stone, from a local bank that was demolished, adds another natural texture to the store's material palette.

The new design not only suits the product and the brand but also provides a degree of greening and sustainability that benefits the community and the consumers who frequent the shop.

Design / 212 Design Inc.; InSite Development, NY
Photography / Courtesy of InSite Development

Japan, as a nation, has not as yet instituted any formal greening regulations for retail stores or commercial buildings. Ichiro Nishi-waki of the Nishiwaki Design Office of Tokyo is endeavoring in any small way possible to bring sustainability and greening into his retail projects. In response to "Is there much effort in Japanese retail design to go green?," the following was the response: "Frankly speaking, especially in retail design, concern for the environment is not enthusiastically adopted as it might be in other areas. First of all, eco-friendly materials or equipment are either more expensive or they are not stylish. Second of all, our clients—apparel manufac-turers and retailers—are not adopting the idea even though we do prepare eco-friendly plans for their approval. The refusal is based on cost or looks."

The Katharine Hamnett brand includes both ecology and nature as part of its core values. However, Nishiwaki felt that if the de-sign was based on using natural materials—in their natural state—the resultant retail setting would look too rustic and not suited to the trendy fashions Hamnett produces. He felt that the "natural" look would not impress or entice the smart and sophisticated young men who are Hamnett's customers. "It is neither stylish or modern" Nishiwaki explains. "Taking advantage of the natural material's qualities of texture and feel, I have blended an image of products with space that enables the brand to impress and attract customers."

The sleek, shiny contemporary open-to-viewing store of under 450 sq.ft. is situated in a commercial building in Tokyo. The look is mainly due to the artificial surfac-

KATHARINE HAMNETT
LONDON

KATHARINE HAMNETT

ing of the natural material. Driftwood and reclaimed railroad ties make up a large part of the materials palette. "They are sliced and painted silver and thus acquire a new face or appearance. In addition, by combining them with other elements—concrete, iron and wires—I tried to create the whole space as an aggregate of the different materials." The driftwood "fence" faces the traffic aisle of the building and continues inside, where it sheathes the perimeter walls of the space. These planks also support the cantilevered hang rods suspended off of them. To complement the silvery sheen of the driftwood and highlight the product presentation, the walls and concrete floors are painted gray and the ceiling is white.

An area of floor-to-ceiling glazing breaks into the rear wall and serves as a display window for another traffic aisle behind the main entrance. Small enclosures—like compact telephone booths with mirror-faced doors—serve as the dressing rooms in the rear corners of the shop. Squares of enclosed space at the front of the shop surround structural columns and also provide on-floor storage space.

"Katharine Hamnett London is a small but challenging step in Japanese retail store design because we are beginning to pay attention to the environment in the retail design area," added Nishiwaki.

Architecture & Design / Nishiwaki Design Office, Tokyo, Japan—Ichiro Nishiwaki, Principal & Creative Director
Photography / Nacasa & Partners, Tokyo

JEAN MACHINE
Yorkdale Shopping Centre, Toronto, ON , Canada

For Rob Whittaker and the design team at RLWDesign, it all came down to "reuse, recycle everything possible" and make it "now and unique." Though Jean Machine's 28 stores are successful, the company wanted a newer, cooler look and attitude. What the client wanted was the attitude, "own your own individual, confident personal style"—and a store design that would articulate that attitude.

In a 19,82sq.ft. space in the Yorkdale Shopping Centre in Toronto, the designers were inspired by Andy Warhol and his Factory's reflective silver interior and Ray Lichtenstein, whose comic book style was used by the Jean Machine's art group to create the wall panels set up over the merchandise display. As Rob Whittaker put it—"a '60s flavor—and unisex."

The very high and very transparent storefront not only allows shoppers to view the store as a whole, but the mall's clerestory windows let daylight stream into the shop as well. The open storefront design, with its mullion-free glazing and the uplit show-case window, revitalized the Jean Machine's presence in the high-end fashion mall. Built

when the economy was free-falling and in the
shortest possible time on a limited budget,
the RLWDesign team reused the client's existing shelves, hang bars, floor fixtures, tables,
accessories and wall standards. The metal bar
shelves were refaced with plastic laminate.
The space is now organized into branded departments that are identified by signage and
the easily changed cartoon graphic panels
that add color to the otherwise silver, white
and chrome palette. Adding sizzle and pizzazz
to the design are the mirrored balls that were
inspired by the silver balloons that were a signature element in Warhol's Factory. They also
recall the disco era and the club-like sound
system in the store contributes as well to the
party-time ambiance.

The designers maximized the interior
height for displays and also increased the on-

floor inventory. Stacking jeans in the ceiling-high open shelving "presents deep inventory/overstock in an orderly and visually interesting manner," Whittaker said. This also did away with the need for a backroom storage area. The side alcove at the rear of the space made it possible to locate the dressing rooms back there while maintaining an open sales space. The spacious changing-room area now has become a "shop, try-on, hang out lounge"—a meeting and stay-awhile space whose large round bench marks a definite meeting place. Located nearby are the Jean Bar and the service desk.

The exposed ceiling and columns were incorporated into the design to affect a warehouse look while the silver-toned vinyl wood floor added shimmer and sheen to the store's silvery look. Adding to the sustainable design, in addition to the reuse and rehabbed materials mentioned previously, is the energy-efficient lighting plan. It includes low-voltage halogens, ceramic metal halides, compact fluorescents and LEDs. This design has gone through seven reincarnations and, as shown here, the brighter and seemingly larger concept has emerged to successfully carry on the Jean Machine brand look.

Design / RLWDesign, Toronto—Rob Whittaker, Principal/Creative Director
Photography / David Whittaker Photography, Toronto

This multi-award winning shop-within-a-shop is located in the Hudson Bay's Vancouver department store. In a space of 5000 sq.ft., the soaring, swirling and staggering shapes and forms create the Olympic Gold shop. The curved fabric-covered frames were designed and fabricated by Eventscape of Toronto in conjunction with HBC's in-house design team. These units provide the dynamic, action-filled surrounding for the Olympic clothing and accessories that were featured in the Vancouver Winter Olympics of 2010.

According to the frame's fabricators, "The challenge on this project was to make a massive structure—the S wall—appear light and 'floating'. To accomplish the feat, three steel-reinforced arches become the main support for the wall." With a decorative element providing support, light aluminum framing formed the rest of the structure. This wall is 70 feet long by 15 feet tall and images of winter sports are graphically expressed across the

wide, attention-getting expanse. Complementing the wall element is a 15-foot-tall column-tree whose curved branches sweep out over 60 feet and heralds the blue and white Olympic signature colors. To complete the total environment there are the unique, fun and intriguing "pod" dressing rooms. Of the same basic framed-fabric construction, these pods have sliding doors that display the word "occupied" in 12 languages when the doors are shut.

As per the client's request, all the above units are modular in design and reusable. They can be repurposed and reskinned to be used in other areas of the store in different configurations. Each segment has hang points

so it can be suspended. In this use, the wall with the three arches serves as the entrance to the shop and the custom millwork incorporates glass, colored acrylic and concealed lighting to illuminate the garments hanging above on the inner side of the wall.

According to the designers at Eventscape, "Almost all our structures are green and always have been. All our elements are prefabricated—eliminating waste on site: they break down into smaller sections thus saving on fossil fuel, and mostly we use aluminum, which has been and can be recycled again after the project. It is also easy to reskin our structures for reuse." The company used earth-friendly materials and the installations are clean and efficient, creating little waste material at the installation site.

The scope, size and shapes of this installation not only succeeded in drawing shoppers to this area, it also garnered numerous design awards—and it is green.

Design / HBC In-House Design Team
Special Elements, Design & Fabrication /
Eventscape Inc., Toronto, ON
Photography / Ed White

"prAna" may roll off the tongue easily but it is a very ancient Sanskrit word that means "breath, life and vitality of spirit." As the company of that name states on its website, "Nature has guided prAna since the very start, with its abundance of color, materials and energy along with endless inspiration to make products that can be well worn and—more importantly—well lived in. We're always looking for new ways to fold sustainable materials and practices into our collections, working to reduce the impact on soils, water supplies and other natural resources."

Since prAna's commitment to the environment "begins at home and extends outward to our retailers and the homes of our employees," it is not surprising that the shops where the fitness, yoga and active outdoor lifestyle clothing for men and women is available are also eco-friendly. For the company's Boulder, CO, flagship store on a pedestrian-friendly and stimulating retail street in the historic district, they called upon the architects and designers at Gensler of San Francisco to create a suitably green store. Located in a

century-old building with 3200 sq.ft. of selling space and a showroom of 2800 sq.ft., the store features numerous green materials: recycled, reclaimed and renewed for use here.

Of special interest are the fixtures that were produced by Laurel Manufacturers of Delanco, NJ. Many were constructed of live-edge walnut slabs from fallen logs and bamboo, which is a readily renewable wood. Laurel proudly proclaims that no tree was cut down to construct these fixtures. In addition to low VOC and mainly water-based glues, resins and finishes—all with no urea formaldehyde in their composition—some of the fixtures have a natural, hand-rubbed oil finish. What appears as an oxidized rust finish on the metal parts is actually 100% biodegradable since no chemicals were used in treating the

metal. In addition, with prAna's involvement, only low VOC and low odor acrylic paints were used on this project.

prAna is part of the Natural Power Initiative (NPI) and its partner 3Degrees , and it supports the U.S.-based wind energy projects. The company purchases renewable energy certificates (REC). The affect of the NPI program is to prevent tons of carbon dioxide from entering the atmosphere. According to prAna's statement, their "commitment assures that renewable energy for our retail locations' usage will be delivered to the electricity grid, the large pools of electricity that we all draw from for our homes and businesses. Simply by supporting renewable energy for our prAna headquarters, all our employees' homes, our two prAna retail locations and 250 of our U.S. retailers, the NPI program will create an environment benefit equivalent to removing over 1677 average cars from the road annually."

"These goals are consistent with our dream here at prAna—to use the brand as a vehicle to create positive change"—and the green and sustainable store is part of that dream's realization.

Design / Gensler, San Francisco, CA
Fixtures / Laurel Manufacturers, Delanco, NJ
Photography / Courtesy of prAna

TIMBERLAND
Westfield Shopping Centre, London, UK

The president and CEO of Timberland, Jeff Swartz, said, "Timberland is committed to reducing global warming and preserving the outdoor environment through the use of more renewable energy, more recycled and reusable materials, less waste, and less chemicals." In the U.S., that means building Timberland stores and exhibits to LEED-CI (commercial interiors) certification standards and in the U.K., where the new Timberland store opened, it means reuse, repurpose and recycle. The over 2500 sq.ft. store is located in London's new Westfield Shopping Centre.

Taking design cues from Timberland's logo, the tree-like roof supports that form. The architecture of the store is constructed of reclaimed timber that stretches across the façade and side elevations as well as climbs the 23+ feet height. These elements, in turn, create unusually shaped display windows

which are furnished with crafted, repurposed furniture and props. Ten-foot doors constructed of salvaged planks create a dramatic entry into the store.

The store interior features signposts and graphic images that visually separate the space by gender; menswear to the right and women's wear to the left. The focal "community totem," in the center of the store, is dedicated to telling how Timberland helps and supports community and environmental projects such as reforestation and special Earth Day events. Throughout the store there is a variety of floor fixtures of varying heights, including display tables of timber stacks with changeable tops, as well as tables and re-

claimed items of furniture which can be mixed and readily moved around in the space. "More than 85% of the materials used in the store have served other purposes in a previous life, with salvaged props and wood from reclaimed or sustainable sources used in flooring and merchandising furniture," said the designers at Checkland Kindleysides, the London-based design consultancy in charge of this project.

Overhead beams draw shoppers to the center of the shop and the footwear display. The two feature walls are covered with Timberland's original boot leather and the curved wall has a dramatic display of footwear. The large-scale outdoor graphic image, featured on the wall, changes with the season. Vintage wooden shoe laths with special brackets make it possible to display various merchandise items at a variety of angles and they appear on a hot steel rolled-back panel.

This space, like other Timberland stores, references local history with photos and graphics that here fill the walls around the changing rooms. Giant graphics of trees and snow-covered mountains paper the walls of the spacious dressing rooms—adding a sense of "being there" and "getting into it!" Ales Kernjak, Timberland's head of store design and visual merchandising said, "This store provides a perfect example of what we stand for as a brand. It reflects our heritage in craftsmanship; our relationship with the outdoors; as well as our environmental values in action. The store front and 'market place' interior design represent Timberland's iconic landmark in the retail field."

Design / Checkland Kindleysides Design Consultancy, London
Photography / Courtesy of Checkland Kindleysides Design Consultancy, London

Peter McIntosh, marketing director for Cowan +Associates, who together with LODA of Montreal and the Timberland Company designed and produced this store, said, "Simplicity and value remain the key attributes for outlet factory store designs, but this does not mean that the outlet store format should overlook opportunities to go green. Sustainable design and outlet centers make a perfect combination. Timberland is stepping things up a notch in retail with its attention to detail that makes their chain of stores—including factory stores—a statement and tribute to conservation and recycling."

This Timberland Factory store in the Deer Park Outlet Mall in Deer Park, NY, has fixtures made from reclaimed iron and other reclaimed materials. Most of the wood used for the fixtures and the wall areas has been reclaimed from the siding and beams of barns that have been destroyed. Throughout the store the floors are stained concrete and only low VOC paints and stains were used. The cash wrap is formed of reclaimed metal that has been forged together to create a functional and attractive green checkout. Fluorescent general lighting and fluorescent recessed and track accent lighting are

used in this store, as well as HID metal halide spots—all to reduce heat emission and save on energy costs.

Occasional area rugs add touches of warmth to the space and the leather lounge chairs are welcoming, friendly and eco-friendly as they break up the areas filled with wall and floor units loaded with Timberland shoes and boots. Bound bundles of recycled and recyclable logs become either display risers, seats or side tables as they reappear throughout the store. Headless forms on low reclaimed wood platforms present the Timberland apparel next to the nested tables upon which the stock is shown. Aside from the large, full-color graphic and the warm colors of the area rugs, the Timberland store is neutral and natural in color and feel.

Bill Morkis, the Cowan + Associates project manager for Timberland Stores, said," Based on all the submissions we have prepared, we expect that the Deer Park store will obtain LEED Gold Certification. Not all projects warrant LEED certification and even small steps further the cause, but either way, it's tremendous to see companies like Timberland dedicated to furthering the movement toward making conservation mainstream in retail. Timberland is committed to its goals to reduce, reuse and repurpose in their ongoing efforts to promote environmental consciousness and further the movement towards greening in retail."

Design / LODA, Montreal, QB, Canada
Architect & MEP Engineer / Cowan + Associates, Worthington, OH
Sustainability Consultant / YRG, NYC
LEED Commissioning Agent / AKF Engineering, NYC
Photography / Keith Taylor, The Timberland Co.

timberland.com

" New Balance's primary objective (for this store) was to commuinicate the brand heritage in technologically innovative products. However, they were also interested in exploring ways to lower the environmental impact of the stores where possible." Eric Daniels, who led the design team at WD Partners, the designers of the New Balance store in Cape Cod adds, "The design team looked for ways to use sustainable products and innovative design features to support the brand."

This prototype store is highly flexible and enhances the brand as well as the presentation of the merchandise; footwear, apparel and accessories. The 3600 sq.ft. space is organized by performance categories and shopping the store is simplified by the use of signage that is visible upon entering the shop. There are areas specified as Men's Fitness, Women's Running, Women's Trail, Girls, Boys, etc. The large-format graphics in the window are printed on recycled paper with green-approved inks and also serve as a background for the in-store merchandising. Flexibility is a vital part of the design and the fixturing system is very adaptable and reconfigurable. It is capable of not only showing footwear but

the appropriate apparel that goes with it. The unique design of these fixtures is that they are designed to use less hardware and make creative use of "software" such as large nylon bands to hold the changeable graphics to the wall fixtures.

Europly, a PSF-certified, non-urea formaldehyde added hardwood plywood was used throughout the store and finished with a low VOC, water-borne clear coating. EcoX, a 70% post-consumer and post-industrial recycled concrete was used for the cashwrap desk. To further the sustainability of the design, a composite board made from waste sunflower husks (Dakota Burl) was used in the construction of the slatwall that appears on some perimeter walls. WD Partners also designed unique display tables that can double as seating benches when cushion pads are attached. Embedded in the concrete floor are differentiating brand messages such as sizes in widths, original shoes for running, etc.

A special focal feature in the center of the store has testing journals and graphic displays. The testing books record stories and testing regimens of real users gathered through "wear test" programs and demonstrate how much effort and innovation goes into the development of New Balance products. They also highlight the technology of the various shoe categories. At the cash/wrap historical photos of New Balance patents

underscore the company's heritage.

The store is pleasantly illuminated with energy-saving, low-voltage fluorescents and spotlights. This store was recognized by A.R.E. (Association for Retail Environments) with a design award for Special Recognition for Green Awareness. As Kirsten Marchand, store planning manager for New Balance was quoted in the A.R.E report, "The intitial barrier [in going green] is the extra time required to understand the green design process and to share the vision with all the project's contributors." It certainly worked at New Balance.

Design / WD Partners, Dublin, OH—Lee Peterson, VP Creative Serviuces; Eric Daniels, Creative Director; Liz Hauswald, Client Project Manager; Chad Niehaus & Christopher Michaels, Prototype Designers
Retailer Team / Kirsten Marchand, Store planning Manager; Stephanie Smith, VP Retail
Architect / Forth Architectural Serviuces, Sandwich, MA—Ron Forth
Photography / Mark Steele Photography, Columbus OH

COLUMBIA SPORTSWEAR
Seattle, WA

The city of Seattle itself has been investing in the promotion of sustainability for some time, which made it an ideal location for this LEED Certified Silver project. The project: a new store for Columbia Sportswear and its premium line of outdoor products. Rachel J. Zsemberg, an associate at Bergmeyer of Boston said, "The sustainability goals of the Columbia Sportswear store in Seattle, WA, were identified early in the project and continually referred to as a benchmark for the direction of the project development through the collective efforts of the entire project team." The store concept was conceived by 2Hemispheres of Clackamas, OR, and the Bergmeyer group of Boston was its architect.

The store's facade of cedar siding and massive timber is located on a busy corner in the downtown area and sets the outdoor scene for the very urban location. Reclaimed and recycled wood are used throughout the shop interior to add not only texture but to create the ambiance of the rustic out-of-doors that in turn will make the city folk feel more like country people. The two levels of the store are connected by a central stairway that envelops an elevator. The walls of this focal piece of architecture are faced with stone that adds another natural, local texture to the

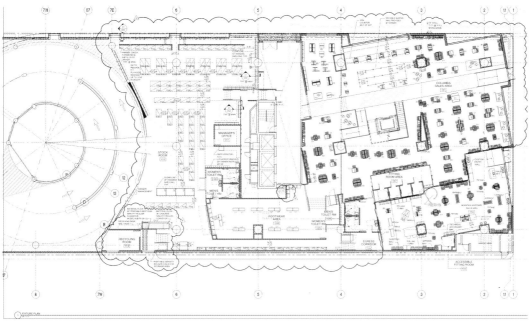

space. The double height of much of the store is enhanced by the soaring, snow-capped graphics and the tall vertical design elements. The overhanging mezzanine level creates low-ceilinged, more intimate shopping spaces on the ground level and the ceilings here are also finished with reclaimed and recycled wood.

The walls of the store are mainly covered with reclaimed wood wall paneling and reclaimed Oak FSC-engineered wood flooring is combined with low VOC carpeting. The wood and metal fixtures also include recycled and reclaimed materials, though they are not specified for the LEED certification. What did help to make this a LEED Silver project was

the 25% in lighting power reduction and the use of daylight-responsive lighting controls within 15 ft. of windows and under the skylights that add natural daylight into the store's lighting plan. Also, more than 95% of construction waste was recycled and 10% of all material that was used had recycled content. A fifth of the material was manufactured regionally, thus cutting down on the energy costs involved in the transportation of the material. In addition to the low VOC carpets, the sealants, paints and adhesives used on the project were also low volatile organic compounds. Water-use reduction technology was used in the toilets.

The woodsy interior is accented with full-color, overscaled graphics and Columbia's signature blue appears on the signage throughout. Dropped shaded lamps are lined up over the multi cashwrap desks that are highlighted by the Columbia blue signs and posters on the back wall. The quotes that appear on the walls add humor and charm as well as underscoring Columbia's attitude toward outdoor living.

Concept & Design / 2Hemispheres, Clackmus, OR Dan Hones
Architecture / Bergmeyer Associates, Boston, MA—Lewis Muhlfelder, Principal in charge; Jeff Paquin, Project Manager; Rachel J. Zsemberg, AA, LEED AP, Associate
Photography / Larry Gill

PLAZA TOO
New York

Plaza Too has an established reputation in its community as a respected family-owned business. According to the designer, Kiku Obata, "Plaza Too brings a sense of family and warmth into each of their stores, making them feel like they are part of the local neighborhood." Kiku Obata & Company, of St. Louis, was commissioned to build on that image while introducing a new brand and store design "that maintains a welcoming and non-intimidating atmosphere while communicating a greater sense of fashion and sophistication."

The new 950 sq.ft. shop is simple, unpretentious and focused on modern fashion. The design is inspired by the individuality and understated glamour of NY's classic department stores and the confident femininity and playfulness of '60s cinema. The design brings a sense of fun and sophistication to the brand experience in a new and modern way. The space's design is interesting and does not

interfere with the presentation of the shoes. By applying a custom wallpaper to the ceiling, the color and pattern seem to visually raise the ceiling height. A fresh, feminine and "organic" feel is given to the space by the color palette of subdued lavenders, cream, yellow and white with effective accents of dark purple and fuchsia. The built-in, armoire-style fixtures allow for vignette merchandising while more shoes are displayed on the illuminated shelves that line the perimeter walls. Adding to the appeal are the wood floors and the sunny, bright yellow cashwrap desk that lends warmth to the space.

Obata also felt that it was imperative that they add sustainable materials to the design. The seating and upholstery fabrics were manufactured at an ISO 14,001 certified facility with heavy-metal-free dyes and reduced emissions. The area rug is made with Invista Antron nylon fibers that are certified by the EPP, and the furniture items were made of woods

that had been harvested in accordance with CITIES (Convention on International Trade and Endangered Species) and constructed with low VOCs and trace formaldehyde.

The result is a great look that suggests ease, intimacy and friendly approachability and it is also sustainable and green—even if the color scheme favors lavender.

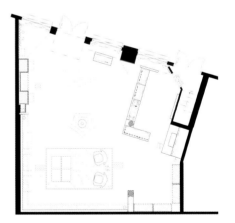

Design / Kiku Obata & Co. St. Louis, MO—Kiku Obata; Russell Buchanan Jr.; Carla Cruz ; Carlos Zamora
Architect / Sarrazin Architecture, Port Chester, NY
Photography / Amy Fletcher, Brooklyn, NY

Who would have thought that the messenger bag—the big, roomy, fabric bag usually worn slung over one shoulder and across the chest—actually has a history and heritage. What started out as a holding container for messengers on bicycles making their way through the hectic traffic of New York City in the '50s has evolved into a designer fashion accessory. This very small shop in the heart of San Francisco's Mission District pays tribute to the bag and offers shoppers the opportunity to select the fabric and pocket configurations and thus create their own personalized messenger bags. Or—as Timbuk2 says, we "create good looking, tough as hell bags you can truly make your own." Timbuk2 considers itself a green company since "while competition is piling up in landfills, we stay on your back—hugging you for a lifetime. So, if you find yourself in a place where you can't possibly love your bag any more—we will give you an out. We'll take your bag off your hands and find it a new (loving) home through Timbuk2's recycling program."

To house and showcase the styles, colors and fabric options, the company's retail store is located in a space of 517 sq.ft. Most of the shop is visible through the glazed front: a pair of windows flanking a metal-framed glass door. The eye-popping red and yellow graphic Timbuk2 logo fills the whole back wall of the shop and camouflages the door that leads to the storage area behind. According to William Duff of William Duff Architects, the San Francisco firm responsible for the design, "a central challenge to the project was to

achieve an iconic look and a sense of depth to the space with a minimalist plan. To achieve this we used a strategy of minimal layering—adding richness to the details." As in the "green-sense"—"less is more," and in this design there is maximum display and brand identity with minimal materials. Low VOC, water-based concrete stain and wall paints were used as well as low maintenance finishes such as board-form concrete plaster walls and the concrete floors. The high-efficiency, low-energy lighting gets a great assist from the natural daylight that comes in through the full glass storefront and the operable clerestory windows, which also enable natural ventilation. Industrial work tables were repurposed and turned into the millwork finished with low gloss, low VOC paint.

By eliminating any extraneous elements, "subtle moves have a more forceful impact. These small moves create a unique retail environment with clarity of purpose that does justice to Timbuk2's vision and brand," said Duff.

Architect / Designer / William Duff Architects, San Francisco, CA—William Duff, AIA, LEED AP & Amelia Dolan
Photography / JD Peterson

Blur, a new eyewear store in Dundas, Ontario, is the ultimate in reclamation. It is the use of reclaimed space, formed out of an alley that existed between two historic buildings in Dundas. The result is a long, narrow "bowling alley" of a store that offers high-end eyewear and personalized service in the 110 ft. by 10-ft. wide space.

Rob Whittaker and his team at RLWDesign divided the long space into five individual/branded studios that are differentiated through the millwork, the finishes and the fixtures. These "studios" create not only a sense of privacy, but add a unique look to the store as a whole and the fashion-forward presentation of the eyewear. The wall colors graduate slightly from darker up front to lighter in the rear where the service desk is located. Throughout, the color feeling is warm and approachable.

One of the main challenges for the designers was creating wall fixtures for this very narrow space. A slim design was required and the facing pairs of fixtures help to define each studio or zone along with two storage cabinets and the central bench. The benches are 26 in. tall—"perching height"—upholstered in pony skin leather and finished with copper-sided tables. These replace the traditional sit-down fitting tables. Shoppers move freely between the benches and the frames in the wall cabinets, making selection a relaxed easy back and forth situation. A square linen covered lampshade highlights each bench location.

The wall cabinets hold a multitude of frames and include built-in mirrors and secure storage space. The mirrors act as decorative frames around the wall units that seem to float in space and also serve the shoppers trying on the eyeglass frames. Frameless tempered glass doors and minimal/concealed hardware do not distract from viewing the merchandise on the wall. The recessed MR16 lamps in the ceiling light up the frames and highlight the shapes and temple details effectively. The decision to go with low-voltage lighting impacted the design cases, which had multiple purposes: showing the frames, acting as a mirror, incorporating thick, luxurious glass shelves—glass is recyclable.

"By bouncing the MR16 lights off the mirrored cases we increased the efficacy of those lights and required far less ambient light," said Whittaker. "The ambient light is provided by 40W A-lamps in oversized shades that give the small but dimmable A-lamp greater volume. Color palettes allow ambient light to carry efficiently throughout a space and reduces the light level required otherwise."

The Canada Green Building Council (CaGBC) has produced LEED Canada, which is an adaptation of the U.S. LEED Green Building rating system. In keeping with the LEED Canada certified ratings, Formica's Real Veneer line was used for the fixtures. The facing material is GreenGuard certified in that it was produced by getting the greatest yield possible from the logs and is factory finished, thus reducing waste and emissions. Natural hides were used to upholster the benches.

Spinneybeck, the leather fabric, has a strong green stance as well: its by-product of the meat industry. The Italian tannery, where it is produced, meets or exceeds all the stringent requirements outlined by government. It is vegetable tanned, outlasts the life cycle of most other upholstery materials and is Green-Guard Certified—no VOC.

The RLWDesign team, under Whittaker, used a graphic approach to the design—repeating squares and cubes: an optical illusion of image repeating in parallel mirrors. The geometric lines were softened by the warm finishes, colors and lighting.

Design / RLWDesign, Oakville, ON, Canada— Rob Whittaker
Photography / David Whittaker Photography, Toronto

ROBERT TALBOTT SHOWROOM
Fifth Ave., New York

Robert Talbott, who founded a tie company with his wife back in 1950, is now an internationally recognized brand name in men's dress shirts, sports shirts, sweaters, leather outerwear and, of course, the ties that began it all. The company has recently added a women's line that is also shown in these quarters. For the company's new showroom on Fifth Ave. in NYC, InSite and 212 Design Inc. of NY, were called upon to make the space fit the brand. Greg Anderson, president of InSite, said, "This was really an inspiring project. Rob is an amazing individual with a fascinating life story and we got to communicate his family's story through the design of this space. Our goal was to combine the brand's rustic Northern California roots with a more refined modern aesthetic—while being mindful of the environment."

In the space there are numerous examples of reuse, repurpose and reclaimed artfully blended with contemporary touches. It starts as the visitor steps off the elevator and is greeted by a pair of reclaimed Indonesian-style doors that are flanked—floor to ceiling—by glass. Reclaimed rustic barn wood, from Vermont, surrounds the reception area and complements the full-wall image of the Monterrey coast line as it appears from the Talbott

Wineries in Carmel Valley, CA. The visitor steps from the limestone entry floor onto the natural sisal carpet in the hallway that leads to the showrooms. The hallway walls tell, in photos, the biography of the brand: Robert Talbott, Travel, Talbott Lifestyle and The Next Generation. Adding decorative accents are the bronze sconces and the original Ansel Adams photograph at the end of the corridor.

Taking advantage of the mostly southern exposure and the generous window placement, natural light counts heavily in the illumination of the showroom. The display walls purposely end two feet from the white painted concrete ceilings and the void is filled with clear glass transoms—to reduce the use of lighting during the daylight hours. As a key element, all concrete beams and columns are clad with reclaimed barn wood. A 40-foot long reclaimed red oak plank table dominates the main men's showroom and serves as a communal selling

area. Resting against one of the barn wood feature walls is a vintage Triumph motorcycle from Robert Talbott's personal collection. The other end of the room carries a dramatic "waterfall tie wall" showcasing over 500 tie styles. Also reused and reinvented for use in the showroom are the three 1930s chandeliers suspended over the communal table. The steel-framed windows were stripped and left unfinished to add another vintage look/texture to the scheme. The perimeter radiated convection system is covered with a three-inch thick countertop of rift white oak and it serves as an extra display surface. The cabinetry is a combination of rift white oak and low VOC white panels trimmed with antique bronze hardware.

Anderson sums up, "We incorporated such environmentally conscious elements, such as using old pieces instead of creating new fixtures where possible, including reclaimed barn wood on the wall and column cladding. The furniture that we had to buy—new or make—was chosen based on sustainability, such as the sisal carpet and the low VOC lacquered display panels. We made the most of natural sunlight to reduce electricity usage."

Design / InSite Design & Development & 212
Design Inc., NYC—Greg Anderson, President
of InSite
Clients / Robert Talbott, Founder; Richard Colen,
President & CEO
Lighting / Lighting Management
Millwork / Modern Woodcrafters
Construction / JRM
Photography / Courtesy of InSite Design &
Development & 212 Design Inc., NYC

Christian Louboutin is a luxury shoe designer and for his showroom in NYC, he called upon the talents of 212Box Architecture of NY to produce a display area that would be functional and chic" With less than one month in which to complete the project, the result is a collection of found objects—furnishings and other items that Christian Louboutin has collected over the years—all orchestrated, arranged and made cohesive by 212Box's concept for the space.

The 3000 sq.ft. space is located in a turn-of-the-last-century building, and it has been divided into a reception area, handbag and shoe display areas, support offices and two conference rooms. The entrance to the showroom is accentuated by found and re-purposed wrought-iron gates. Immediately viewed upon entering the lobby is a crisp white wall with the supersized, designer's logo in the company's signature red color. This entry zone is furnished with furniture from Louboutin's personal collection. A feature

wall, behind the reception desk and leading down the hallway to the showrooms, is filled with pressed, dried and framed leaves collected by Louboutin in Cairo.

Found in a salvage shop and resurrected and restored by the 212Box team are the stained-glass panels that once graced the American Airlines Terminal in the JFK airport. Also reused here are some other stained-glass windows that are combined with vintage large brass doors that have also been reclaimed for this showroom. Maximizing the space in the handbag and shoe display areas are the red rolling storage units that were custom designed for this purpose along with the mirrored millwork.

Eric Clough, principal at 212Box said, "This was an intense design/build contract where we sourced used materials, found objects and reused existing furniture throughout the entire space. The only new walls that were built were two offset walls, each lined with mirror on one side. The parallel walls reflect and divide the space in a fluid, ever-changing way when experiencing/walking around."

The result is a highly personal and efficient space: one that reflects the interests and collections of the founder and designer—Christian Louboutin—while providing a beautiful and glamorous background for his products. In its reusing and repurposing of the various found and reclaimed items, it brings a degree of greening into the attractive design.

Architecture & Design / 212Box Architecture, NY
Design Team / Eric Clough, Eun Sunchun, Robert Mastic, Jennifer Broutin, Patsi Vienravi, Michela Chiavi, Tania Chau
Photography / © 2009 Tom Powel Imaging

Here today and now—but only a memory in a few weeks. Fortunately, this retail pop-up shop has been digitally recorded and the memory can be shared with future architects and designers who have a green agenda.

Jean Pierre Veillet is a Portland, OR-based artist, designer and builder. Trained as a sculptor, Veillet takes a spatially informed, socially conscious and aesthetically thoughtful approach to projects from tiny retail renovations to ground-up eco-developments. He is intrigued by the intimacy that can be created between people and their environments, and by the possibilities of social engineering on a much larger scale. Though most of his work is intended to last for decades or more, he accepted the challenge to create the Nau store in Soho which disappeared after six weeks.

Following is the press release from the

Nau company which explained it all. "Veillet's Manhattan project is a 'pop-up,' a type of temporary store that has become a sign of the times in cities that have experienced higher-than-usual retail vacancy rates. During a pop-up's brief lifespan, a store is designed, built, used, disassembled, and discarded—with many of the materials ending up in landfills. Instead of throwing away items, Veillet opted for an ecological approach."

The following is how Veillet explained what he did and how he did it." I accepted the challenge of designing the temporary retail outlet in Soho for the clothing company Nau using whatever materials I could find. Utilizing my sculpture background and the visual vocabulary contained in found objects, I set out to create a warmer and welcoming vision of the Nau branded store. Scraps of wood, metal,

cardboard and cable were reclaimed from the city's waste stream. Discarded or underutilized items were found along train tracks, on sidewalks, on the sides of roads, and random items found abandoned in warehouses, etc., were repurposed and reused. My entire materials budget to fill in and complete the space was $4500, which to put things in perspective, is much less than what one light fixture can cost in a traditional retail build-out. We completed the project in 20 days. We had 10 days to gather materials and build the fixtures off-site, and another ten days to install the fixtures and complete the interior build out after taking possession."

And now—back to Nau's press release: "The end result: Designer-quality clothing racks fashioned from metal pipes, casters, old beams and tense cable. Ceilings were fashioned from tree limbs, furniture derived from sheets of thrown-away cardboard, discarded crates and repurposed ladders." Veillet has the next-to-the-last words: "This was a project that played into many of my interests and passions. It was a performance piece, or a short film made up of social interaction,

RECYCLED **POLYESTER**

WHAT WE DO

> Our synthetic fabrics – hard shells, soft shells, linings – are made from recycled polyester.

WHY SHOULD YOU CARE?

> It comes from a blend of post-consumer and industrial materials – recycled plastic bottles and other polyester fabrics – that would otherwise end up in the landfill.

> Recycled polyester uses one third less energy than virgin polyester.

> It's durable, and, via a closed loop recycling process, can be reused continuously.

TRY IT ON.

design process, activism, and the luck that comes with the brew."

In this smart, stylish, sophisticated town—filled with exquisite fashion boutiques and retail palaces—it was a ramshackle, run-down, patched together piece of urban sculpture that the NY press and the local magazines devoured. One magazine, Cool Hunting, summed it up with—"Elegantly contrasts the warmth of the materials with the white walls and floor of the existing architecture and gorgeously ties in with the stunning exposed wood ceiling beams and rear sky lights."

Veillet uses his creativity—and imagination—to reuse, repurpose, reclaim and eventually recycle "found" materials that were lost until he finds a new use and a new life for them in one of his unique designs.

Design / Jean-Pierre Veillet of Siteworks, Portland, OR
Photograpy / Courtesy of Siteworks

A Statement From LOHAS
(Lifestyle Of Health & Sustainability)

The past few years have seen the rise in consciousness of the impact people's purchasing decisions have on the environment. This demand has brought about the transformation of sustainability initiatives to be considered mandates for companies. Not only do companies need to show they are complying with sustainable policy, but exceeding it by leaps and bounds. Those that are not integrating this process into their overall business plans are not only missing dramatic energy and waste savings, they are also missing a significant amount of consumers who would otherwise be advocates for their products— i.e. the early adopter LOHAS consumers. —*Ted Ning, executive director, LOHAS*

"Spearheading Environmental Management—in Germany"
Contrary to America, the landscape of Germany has a high density of population. The roll-out of one-way packaging in the '60s and '70s, in combination with the "economic miracle" of the Federal Republic in the '80s, started the "Green Party" as a protest-movement against garbage in the countryside and waste-disposals or waste-burning. Government reacted by establishing a Federal Minister for Environmental. At the end of '80s Prof. Dr. Klaus Toepfer shaped the German Packaging Law; later he spearheaded the "Kyoto Protocol." Changing his position to work for the UN, he was succeeded by Dr. Angela Merkel—today German chancellor. Having the EU-Presidency in 2008, Merkel put the environment onto the agenda at the G8 Meeting. Retailers—being very sensitive to consumer trends—reacted proactively and became drivers for change.

As pro-environmental action is a question of all steps within the total supply chain— not to absorb "positive" activities by "negative" actions—the European Retail Academy developed in 2008 a flowchart for Environmental Retail Management. It starts at the level of agriculture and ends with consumers—LOHAS (Lifestyle of Health and Sustainability). Following the inductive way of research—and also to give retailers and suppliers a high degree of individuality—the flow chart is at this stage just monitoring and not evaluating each activity, because first the methodology of measuring CO_2 output, etc., has to be agreed on. Retailers can break down percentages of a total of 100 percent of their own "company efforts" to all steps of the flow-chart. That data is published as a panel to reflect the status of the retail-industry. Due to publication, this inspires retail for competition in this field—also promoted by an annual EHI Retail Institute Energy Award. It might be that Environmental Retail Management becomes one of the most important marketing tools in the decade ahead.

—Prof. Dr. B. Hallier / Hallier is Managing Director at the EHI Retail Institute,
President of the EuroShop exhibition and President of the European Retail Academy.

Outdoors + Health + Equipment

The outdoor goods retailer, REI, believes that "engaging with and respecting the environment is a core principle of most outdoor adventures and it should be a fundamental part of the shopping experience." Brian Unmacht, REI's senior vp of sales and store development, said "our increased focus on green buildings and the community began with our Seattle flagship store in 1996. Since then we continued to develop stores that represent our dedication to the outdoors by reducing the environmental impacts of such buildings and helping to inspire outdoor recreation. Boulder (this store) helped bring our commitment to the next level, representing a new REI standard for sustainability."

This 42,000 sq.ft. store in Boulder, CO, is a renovation and expansion of an existing building. The store, according to the designers at Gensler of San Francisco who were responsible for the new look, was designed as a working laboratory to analyze the performance of green building features and new retail concepts. Another part of the challenge was to raise the bar in terms of how the REI store and brand experience could better serve the community—and the environment.

The overall design is based on nature and that concept is reflected in the exterior architecture and the interior design elements. The façade picks up visual cues from its surroundings—"earthern strata, thick forest canopies and towering pinnacles," Unmacht said. Throughout the interior filled with a color and material palette inspired by the terrain, natural elements appear as graphic reminders that this is an outdoor experience store. Skeletal tree shapes greet the shopper in the vast entry hall where the forms are backed up by cubistic piinnacles—reminders of what appeared on the façade. The outlined, stylized trees also appear as a broad fascia design in

the shoe area. Truncated, cone-shaped lamp shades of fabric stretched over metal frames are suspended down to accentuate certain areas and lined up dramatically in the entry hall.

The elevated community center is in the center of the store and is free of merchandise, The 2000 sq.ft. space is solely dedicated to be a resource for the community to learn about the outdoors and the opportunities to protect shared natural spaces as well as provide a venue for events, presentations and demonstrations. This glass-enclosed space is also defined by the graphic tree motif in white on the glazed surface. This focal area serves as an organizational core around which the ap-

parel zones are collected.

Gensler's team designed new and efficient fixtures for this REI store so that the vast and varied collection of product can be properly presented, from kayaks and tents to apparel and granola. Wherever possible, recycled and recyclable materials were used, including reclaimed wood, stone, rubber flooring and Marmorette linoleum. Plyboo, made of readily replemishable bamboo, was used, as was recycled fiber board. Low VOC paints and adhesives were used as needed. While incorporating green elements in the building's construction, one of the technologies required aggressive daylight harvesting systems that

would reduce the store's energy consumption by allowing more natural day light use over in-store lighting. To accomplish this, the architects used highly reflective, funnel-shaped tubes—Solar Tubes—to channel daylight from the roof throughout the store. This saves about 20% of the energy costs. Also, a light monitor lets in the sunlight while capturing the sun's energy. That powers the store through a technology called Building Integrated Photovoltaics (BIPV). The use of the solar roof monitor in this store is the first use of this technology in a retail environment.

In addition to gaining a LEED CI Certification, this store has been recognized with numerous awards and citations, including Chain Store Age's "Store of the Year for Environmental Sustainability." "REI challenged us to raise the bar in terms of how their store and brand experience could better serve the community and the environment. The new store design creates a sense of community for both REI's members and non-members, and reflects REI's leadership in environmental design," said Ted Jacobs, Gensler's design director/principal.

Architect & Store Design / Gensler, San Francisco, CA—Ted Jacobs, Design Principal; Ray Shick, Principal; Zsofia Kondor, Project Manager; Bill Nelson, Project Architect; Karen Skillin, Job Captain/ Project Manager; Daniel Gonzales, Job Captain; Vivian Volz, Specifier
REI (Recreational Equipment, Inc) / In-House Design team
Solar Power & Renewable Energy / Solar Design Associates,San Fran. CA
Photography / Benny Chan

When the designers at the JGA design firm of Southfield, MI, were signed to design the new The North Face in Boise, ID, the design objective was clear: "To create a retail environment designed around performance technology, pride of heritage in The North Face brand, and a sense of sustainability by developing the store interior as certified by the U.S. Green Building's Council's LEED program—targeting a gold level certification." Sustainability and conservation are core values of The North Face and their pledge is "to advance the well-being of the planet." The company also "aggressively and responsibly continues to integrate environmental, economic, philanthropic, and social innovations into their business practices"—and JGA had to accommodate and point all this up in their design.

The building that houses this 7,7500 sq.ft. operation is well over 100 years old and the façade has been painted a rustic version of The North Face signature red, so that the building will blend in with the surrounding red brick structures. The first two floors are now used for retail space and what was originally two separate areas has now been unified by an airy and spacious atrium stairway. The open feeling of the atrium staircase helps downplay the low ceiling height. Windows on the second floor that had been blocked off for more than half a century were "opened" and

outfitted with high-efficiency glazing. The daylight now streams in, complemented by the passive solar heating provided for the store.

Since the major part of the selling is done on the second level, prominent focal and visual elements are used to attract shoppers on the ground level and lead them up to the main merchandise presentation. Leading the shoppers is the large graphic mural that greets them and the dramatic footwear wall. Socializing and community involvement are encouraged in the community area and a specific zone was created with custom-made bins especially created for the recycling of products by The North Face associates.

Recycling, repurposing and reuse were all part of the design agenda and used during the restoration process. The original wood joist ceilings were uncovered and their artisan-crafted nature contributes warmth to the space and help to visually raise the low ceilings. The fixtures that were specified are all sustainable in nature and though some new materials were introduced, many—like the bamboo plywood (Plyboo)—were also used in previous The North Face stores. The Plyboo was also used for the back-room storage

shelving and the wood that is used on the feature wall is recyclable and certified as grown and harvested using sustainable guidelines as is the timber used for the flooring. SkyBlend, a wood particle board that was also used here, is composed of pre-consumer recycled wood fiber and manufactured without any added formaldehyde. The back area flooring is made of recycled vinyl content and installed with a low VOC adhesive. All the paints that were used to affect the warm and pleasant ambiance are acrylic with less odor and low VOC," said Ken Nisch, AIA, chairman of JGA. "Green is about recycle, reclaim, repurpose and lastly—respect. The North Face in Boise, which achieved gold level LEED Certification, is intelligent in its use of high performance HVAC, lighting and the use of natural day lighting within its environment. It is also respectful in that it reclaimed, repurposed and restored many of the elements of the 1890's building using the structure's own timber construction and brick and stone shell—two advantages that are environmentally friendly, brand right, and provide a warm and textural setting to the North Face's technical products."

Design / JGA, Southfield, MI—Ken Nisch, Chairman; Mike Curtis, Creative Director; George Vojnovski, Project Manager
Client Team / Lindsay Rice, VP of Retailing; Bernie Bishop, Director of Visual Merchandising; Rick Marini, Director of Stores
Photography / Laszlo Regos Photography, Berkley, MI

For the Bergmeyer design organization of Boston, undertaking the design of the L.L. Bean 25,000 sq.ft. store in Mansfield, MA, meant adapting a prototype it had already developed to expand the company's retail program as well as encompass several new objectives. These objectives included providing interactive and educational services for L.L. Bean's customers; making a positive connection with the shoppers; embodying the L.L. Bean values; developing a sense of community; responding to regional influences and connecting with the local environment. It also meant creating a sustainable retail environment. Ken Kacere, senior vp and general manager of retail for L.L. Bean said, "L.L. Bean has a strong commitment to protecting and preserving outdoor space. Because of this commitment, it is important for the company to create a sustainable retail environment for our customers."

The store is warm, inviting and earthy/outdoorsy, thanks to its abundant natural materials and reclaimed wood. The façade resembles a ski lodge—or a frontier town cityscape—with its long walkway sheltered by a wooden overhang. The floor-to-ceiling windows allow full and frequent looks into the store interior. On the inside, the raw wood skeletal structures and dividing walls, the

focal displays on nesting tables, the occasional and welcoming sitting areas furnished with rockers and Adirondack chairs, and the merchandise set out in easy to see, select and coordinate clusters, make shopping this L.L. Bean store a pleasurable experience. There are clearly defined and wide circulation paths that add to the adventure and the comfort of shopping in this sprawling space. The numerous clerestory windows from the upper reaches—combined with the large display windows—fill the space with natural light for most of the day.

In order to include as many sustainable or eco-friendly features as possible in the store's design and construction, the custom fixtures were constructed of reclaimed wood and steel, and recycled content carpet and rubber flooring were installed. Reclaimed wood and old barn boards were also used for the wall paneling and the paints and adhesives used contained minimal volatile organic compounds (VOC). 94% of the reduced construction debris that was produced was sent to recycling facilities. The use of natural materials and L.L. Bean's commitment to meeting LEED standards exhibited the company's willing-

ness to accept responsibility for the environment, and also served as an encouragement for their customers to become involved in the "outdoor community." The store recently received LEED Silver certification because in addition to all the aforementioned practices, the designers were able to incorporate natural daylight and also reduce energy use by 40% over comparable stores of this size by the use of state-of-the-art lighting control systems, occupancy sensors and an energy use management system. By LEED standards, the design also scored high on innovative design as well as materials and resources.

Learning spaces are located throughout, especially in the bicycle and fly fishing departments, and there are in-store "clinics" for the shoppers' benefit. Shopping the store is a "positive experience" and all that L.L. Bean wanted it to be—as well as a sustainable design.

Architecture & Design / Bergmeyer, Boston, MA
LEED Consultant / Indoor Air Services
Lighting Design / LAM Partners
Photography / Richard Mandelkorn

TREK BICYCLE STORE
Peachtree City, GA

The 12,000 sq.ft., two-level Trek Bicycle store is a fine example of a commercial-retail building and store interior that takes steps toward sustainable design by implementing green elements. Cowan + Associates of Worthington, OH, was the architect/designer for this project situated in upscale residential Peachtree City, GA. The Trek Bicycle Corporation is an environmentally conscious manufacturer and marketer of bicycles, accessories and apparel—"promoting consciousness toward the environment is inherent in the culture surrounding Trek Bicycles."

The Trek store takes up 6000 sq.ft. of the main entry level and as designed and laid out by the team at Cowan+ Associates, it consists of a series of individual shops. This boutique concept takes away the overwhelming feeling often felt when a shopper is not really sure what type of bicycle he or she wants to get. The store is divided into areas dedicated to and merchandised for leisure, hybrid and kid bicycles, as well as those for professional road riders and mountain bike enthusiasts. "The shop-within-a-shop concept allows for a simple shopping experience and more personal attention," said Peter McIntosh, marketing director at the design firm. "It is also important to Trek that environmentally forward material be used in their store in order to stay in keeping with its environmentally focused corporate culture, and also to be reflective of its core customer's lifestyle while at the same time maintaining a budget for independent dealers."

The building is steel and CMU block framed with mortar studs. The façade is finished with cultured stone and three of the exterior walls are filled with windows designed to allow natural daylight into the space. Along with the fact that the building was positioned on the plot to take advantage of the day lighting, the interior is equipped with an energy efficient, automatic day-light controlled general and accent lighting plan. The lighting scheme includes metal halides,

LED and fluorescent fixtures. For the interior finishes, low VOC paints and carpeting were used and recycled rubber flooring is used throughout. The floor fixtures and bike rack systems are metal and unseen but felt—and green—are the HVAC system and the lavatory fixtures.

Eva Knutson, creative/ design director for Cowan + Associates, adds, "Going green with construction initially can cost a bit more up front, but retailers will see payback over time from energy and water conservation efficiencies, employee health and productivity gains, and lower maintenance costs. Conservation is impacting and will continue to impact the future of all decisions regarding retail construction."

This design was not commissioned for LEED or any other green certification, though sustainability played a major role in the design and construction. Over 100 Trek dealers around the world are remodeling or opening new stores based on this store's design and strategies—receiving varying levels of green elements based on budget and store type.

Architecture & Store Design / Cowan + Associates, Worthington, OH
Photography / Courtesy of The Bicycle Center/ Trek Store of Atlanta

BEST BUY

John Hancock Center, Michigan Ave., Chicago IL.

In describing the new Best Buy store in the John Hancock Center in Chicago, Monica Salamon, Best Buy's general manager, said, "This truly is a community store and we are excited to finally bring Best Buy to one of the world's premier tourist attractions." Located in 30,000 sq.ft. of space on the first and second levels of this towering structure and surrounded by a massive array of windows, the store becomes "a landscape of technology floating inside a glass and steel box," according to Charles Sparks, founder of the design

firm that bears his name and creator of the store's interior design.

The design of this store is an evolution from the urban format created by Charles Sparks + Company for Best Buy's "flagship store experience" on upper Broadway in NYC in 2007. In this location, the concept is "letting the inside out," with partial-height fixtures and walls with bold graphics facing the street and visible through the many windows. These windows let daylight stream into the store and fill both levels with light.

The murals are of Chicago landmarks and neighborhoods—making it feel like a local shop rather than a national chain. Working with the architect, Stan Weisbrod, a custom designed, open-rise stairway connects the two levels and the well opening between the floors is "alive from the activity of people, natural daylight and the focal location along the grand 'esplanade' aisle of the second floor." A casual seating area, up here, offers shoppers a place to rest, revive and enjoy the surroundings that are filled with the latest technology,

entertainment products and services to benefit them at work and at play. Getting around the two levels is simplified by the simple but decorative and informative signage lettered in white on the blue clad columns and on the perimeter panels. The color scheme is limited to the Best Buy blue, with white, gray and silver. The blue carpeted floor complements the off-white walls and ceilings.

A Best Buy company statement says, "As a company, we aspire to be environmentally, socially and financially accountable to our

brands and business operations worldwide. We are focused on the environment for a number of reasons. First, we understand that the natural resources we rely on to run our business is finite. Second, we are aware of the growing environmental impact of consumer electronics. And ultimately, we care about people and the planet and know consumers and our employees care too. We are committed to do our part to be a leader in such areas as recycling and developing and selling energy efficient products. Many of our customers want to know that the products they buy from us are responsibly made and sourced. They want perspective on energy efficient and environmentally responsible technology, choices that save resources and money. They want confidence that their old electronics are recycled, refurbished and not dumped in a landfill. They want our stores to be efficient and sustainable." Best Buy is one of only a handful of retailers to have their prototypical store plans certified by the USGBC at Silver level under the Volume Certification program.

While the Michigan Avenue store is certainly not a prototypical Best Buy store, Sparks and Weisbrod made sure that this new, sleek and smart blue-and-white store is also

checkout

caja registradora

FREE phone upgrade

Ask us how

at&t

green. The excellent lighting plan includes energy-saving elements such as lighting controls and occupancy sensors, LED track lighting in the specialty areas and energy-efficient, recessed can lights and T-5 fluorescent ceiling fixtures throughout the store. In addition to the low volatile organic compound (VOC) paints and sealants, the designers specified carpet tiles that passed the Carpet & Rug Institute Green label for low VOC emissions. Special floor mats, at the entry, capture dirt and keep other particles from entering the building. The terrazzo that was used on the staircase (an electrical energy saver when compared to an elevator or escalator) was manufactured locally and also has low VOC epoxy binders and significant longevity and low maintenance costs. Finally, the loose fixtures that are on the floor used low urea formaldehyde MDF boards for their construction. Of course, the demolition was carried out in accordance with the Demolition Site Waste Recycling ordinance and all efforts were made for water conservation.

Their customers want and expect Best Buy to be green and that is what they got in this new store on the Miracle Mile in Chicago.

Interior Design / Charles Sparks + Company, Westchester, IL—Charles Sparks, Principal; David Koe, Senior Creative Director; Stephanie Moore, Director of Visual Communications
Architect of Record / SJW Architects & Associates, Oak Park, IL—Stanley Weisbrod, AIA, LEED AP
For BEST BUY / Brendon Stuckey, Development Manager; Tony Harms, Store Design & Planning Supervisor
Photography / Charlie Mayer Photography, Oak Park, IL

With the Verizon Wireless stores (VZW) in Casper, WY, and in Avondale, AZ, the major design goal was to demonstrate to the national and area VZW real estate/store design teams and corporate shareholders that 'green' stores could be built without a significant impact to the cost of the store project, the customer experience or look and feel of the brand. Based on Verizon's Evolution (EVO) prototype design that was developed by the Gruskin Group of architects and designers of Springfield, NJ, the concept was adapted to be more "green" and to reduce its impact on the environment. This was accomplished by Gruskin working closely with VZW's internal "green" task force and Paladino and Company, which served as the sustainability consultant.

The 3,479 sq.ft. store in Casper's Eastridge Mall is not only the first VZW retail store to apply for LEED certification but is be the first LEED Gold certified store in Casper. "Our new green store in Casper provides plenty of space both for shopping and customer service, in keeping with our commitment to deliver innovative voice and data plans, exciting new

devices and services, and the best possible wireless experience," said Melanie Braidich, the regional President of Verizon Wireless. The store offers consumers and small-business customers hands-on interaction with wireless voice, data, music and video services in the shiny, clean and open space. Though the store is green and was constructed with recycled content materials—half of which were produced regionally, made use of Energy Star equipment and had a lighting power 56% less than required by ASHRAE 90.1 standard—the overall impact is of the signature red color that pops out over and over again. It starts as the beckoning call on the façade and accentuates the otherwise gray/neutral interior space. The use of reduced low VOC paints, combined with Green Label Plus carpeting and GreenGuard system furniture not only racked up LEED certification points but added to the comfortable and welcoming feel of the space. Here shoppers may sample a large number of fully activated new phones and devices first hand. As they move through the uncluttered store,

they are free to stop at one of the several hands-on fixtures or sit down at one of the seats offered in front of on-line computers. The red highlighted perimeter walls are also filled with "try me" apparatuses and on one side, in an alcove, is a bank of service stations manned by helpful VZW associates there to assist shoppers, answer questions or accept payments from clients.

The store prides itself on how it has reduced its impact on climate change through the reduction of energy use and its use of ozone-friendly refrigerants. VZW's Hopeline program recycles unwanted wireless phones and equipment, thus reducing e-waste from entering landfills. Also, 56% of the construction waste in building this store was diverted from landfills. The company is so proud of what it has accomplished in greening and sustainability that it has implemented a "green" education program. The staff is trained to conduct educational tours in the store, pointing out the green features in the space and their impact on the environment.

Designer/Architect / Gruskin Group, Springfield, NJ—Kenneth A. Gruskin, AIA, PP, CID
Mechanical & Electrical Engineers / Henderson Engineers
Sustainability Consultant / Paladino and Company
Photography / Kenneth A Gruskin

It all began with a passion for skin care and the benefits of aromatherapy. When Emily Davidson Hoyt, a long-time sufferer of migraines and sensitive to synthetic ingredients in cosmetics, found relief in the use of natural ingredients and aromatherapy, she decided to create her own line of pure and natural products. The result—the Lather shop!

Alex Soto, the creative director and partner in The Retail Element, a design and branding company in Pasadena, said, "When Lather approached us to design their new concept, we approached the retail concept in line with their mission statement. They use all-natural and environmentally friendly ingredients and do not do any testing on animals. We wanted to create a wonderful, relaxing and educational experience for the customer. We designed the store to be easy to shop and to test all the products."

The space is located in Old Town Pasadena, and the heavily timbered ceiling of the old structure is visible through the numerous openings in the dropped ceiling. Elements in the dropped ceiling seem to float—soft, rounded and cloud-like—over the mainly white and gentle pastel-toned interior. The all-white fixtures and the feminine and fresh peach and mottled sky blue accents are complemented by the bamboo flooring and

the numerous live plants, dried spiraling branches and the twigs embedded in the plastic panels. The peach-toned columns serve as focal elements for the rounded tables and counters that envelop them. Adding brilliant touches of color are the framed illustrations of the natural ingredients used in Lather's products that appear on the wall. The textured wall treatment and the glass boxes filled with the actual natural ingredients turn the branding wall into a visual draw. "The branding wall was designed to educate the customers as to the natural and environmentally friendly ingredients used by displaying the actual raw materials in display cases," Soto said.

In selecting the building, finishing and furnishing materials, Soto and his partner, Scott Kohno, chose mainly sustainable and eco-friendly materials. The main flooring material is a strand-woven bamboo flooring because it is a natural, renewable resource that is a grass—not a wood product—and is harvested every five years. A solid surface material, Avonite, made of recycled factory scraps, was used for the counter tops as well as a microchip agglomerate with seashells that is produced by Architectural Systems, Inc. These contribute to LEED Certification, as do the decorative panels used on the floor

fixtures and wall displays that are made of natural thatch embedded in plastic. It is a reclaimed/recycled product from 3-Form. To cut down on energy consumption but still maintain a bright dramatic effect, metal halide spot lighting is featured in the lighting plan. For the inviting and relaxing furniture, special bent-bamboo lounge seating was added to the design scheme. The design concept also included a plan to encourage shoppers to recycle the used product packaging and containers for future store credits. There is also a Lather Recycle Bin visible to all at the point-of-sale.

Soto added, "Lather store as a 'green retailing' concept takes in all aspects of the environment—from the basic mission statement, product make up and educational experience to the environmentally friendly materials used in construction." Natural products in a natural setting.

Design / The Retail Element, Pasadena, CA—Alex Soto, Creative Director, Partner; Scott Kohno, Partner
Lather Team / Emily Davidson Hoyt & Robert Hoyt, Owners; Matt Heinze, Visual Merchandiser
Photography / Dale Wilcox

LE LABO
Elizabeth St., New York

This little store was created to feel like a cross between an old fashioned apothecary and a modern laboratory. On Elizabeth St. in NYC's hip Nolita district, the shop specializes in made-to-order scents, as well as pre-packaged toiletries originally created by the two scent wizards who own the Le Labo brand label. Edouard Roschi and Fabrice Penot had a vision of making and selling perfumes that are freshly hand-made and personalized with the client's name and the date on the antique-looking label. To create their concept shop, they called upon Eric Romeo and the Auric Consulting and Design firm of NYC to make their vision a reality.

Much has been reused and repurposed in the 530 sq.ft. space. As viewed through the window, set above the almost raw concrete based front, the store has a split personality; a blend of old and new. The shopper steps up onto the industrial stamped metal entry tread. The next move is onto the richly colored and textured reclaimed wood floor—distressed and worn by time and foot traffic. The ancient embossed tin wall faces the left side wall and it has been restored and refreshed with silver paint. The opposite wall reclaims the original brick wall now finished in a laboratory white to

complement the simple contemporary counter/work surface that fills most of the right side of the space. The display tables that are set against the tin wall are constructed of old pieces of metal—fashioned anew. Old chairs and furniture make a welcome rest area in the rear of the shop

Eric Romeo, of Auric Consulting and Design who has also produced variations on this theme for Le Labo around the world, said, "Developing the architectural brand design for Le Labo was fundamentally informed by the concept of reuse. With each step in the development process, we asked ourselves how we could minimize our impact on the environment and the budget through reclamation. By gently probing and observing the existing space, we discovered elements such as the antique tin panels behind the existing gyp-

sum board panels. These beautiful tin panels were then incorporated into the language of the Le Labo brand. The existing floors were also retained but manipulated with the force of swinging chains to create a distressed patina that is also carried on in Le Labo stores throughout the world.

"I am convinced that approaching this project with sensitivity to the existing space and observing what it had to offer us by the reuse succeeded in establishing a rock-solid brand design and paved the way for the global expansion of Le Labo."

Design / Edouard Roschi & Fabrice Penot
Architecture & Construction / Auric Consulting
& Design, NY—Eric Romeo, Principal
Photography / Giorgia Martone

LIVING PERFUME

Henri Bendel, Fifth Ave., New York

Henri Bendel, the Fifth Avenue specialty store, launched an innovative, pop-up, interactive exhibit on its third floor. The exhibit featured the perfumes, craft and collection of Mandy Aftel, a leading natural perfumer. This exhibit was used to introduce Aftel's newest fragrance, Lumiere.

The design was created by the talents at Brandimage, Desgrippes Laga of NY in conjunction with Cheryl Heller of Heller Communications design, also of NY. They worked closely with Henri Bendel's executive team. The concept was "to invite consumers to smell Aftel's natural fragrances and materials and then respond by creating their own unique 'scent portraits,' in essence making a picture of their own sense of the universal natural smell that they can take away, and that will then become part of the exhibition." As the designers noted, "taken together, these 'crowd sourced' portraits will represent an aggregated view of consumers' intimate perceptions of scent."

Explaining the design of this presentation, Jeremy Dawkins, executive creative director of Brandimage, Desgrippes Laga, said, "Sculptural forms made from smooth, silhouetted layers of white sustainable eco board suggest the sensuality of natural elements—trees, stone formations, a forest path—while paral-

Design / Brandimage, Desgrippes Laga, NY—
Jeremy Dawkins, Executive Creative Director
In Conjunction with Heller Communications
Design, NY Cheryl Heller, Creative Advisor
Architect / Maki Schmidt
Fixtures / AS Custom
Eco Materials / EA International
Installation / Novo Arts
Produced by / Sensory Runway
Photography / Brandimage, Desgrippes & Laga

leling the layers of perfume and invoking the mystery and beauty of scent." The space was designed to "impose itself into the store environment in the way a tree would grow in a busy urban street." One of the major problems for the designers was to draw shoppers up to the third floor and into the exhibit—away from "that glorious atrium." To affect the "forest" of multi-layered, cut-out tree forms and fixtures that frame the atrium area, E-Core Plus (EC+) boards, made of recycled materials and organic glues, and Xanite, recycled post consumer and 100% repulpable materials, were combined with the most advanced digital printing/cutting technologies.

After this use, some of the units were converted into fixtures in Bendel's bookstore. Other parts will be reused as needed for future exhibit rentals.

Julie Anixter, the design firm's chief marketing officer said, "We were gratified by the response to an eco-friendly, pop-up retail exhibit. This experiential in-store exhibition is as multi-layered—literally and figuratively—as Aftel's fine, all-natural perfumes. What resulted was an environment that was surprisingly fresh and impermanent and provided a stunning contrast between fixtures and furniture and the formal, historic landmark Henri Bendel environment."

NUSTA SPA
Washington, DC

Not only is the Nusta Spa in Washington, DC, a place that is kind, refreshing and reclaims the body's energy of the men and women who partake of what the spa has to offer, it is also kind, thoughtful and reclaims elements and respects nature and the world. This 5000 sq.ft. spa includes a retail/reception area, consultation space, seven treatment rooms, lockers and specialty salons—and it was the first spa to earn LEED Gold Certification for its eco-friendly construction and practices.

Created by Envision Design of Washington, DC, the design draws its inspiration from the ancient Incan culture of Peru. Even the name "Nusta" means "royalty" in the Quechua language. In describing the project, Kendall Wilson, the principal of the design company, said, "Sight, sound, smell and touch are all integrated in the design of the space in a highly refined manner. A large limestone wall in the reception area recalls the construction of Machu Picchu, while angled reveals inspired by the vast lines of the Nazca Plateau are applied to accent walls. Clusters of soy candles illuminate alcoves and crisply detailed bamboo slats are applied to the treatment room ceilings. An indoor waterfall provides a soothing atmosphere to the relaxation area while patrons sip herbal

tea. An 11-foot wall of oak boards milled from reclaimed structural timbers defines the separation between public and private spaces."

A painted blue ceiling, indirectly illuminated, floats over the corridor that leads to the treatment rooms turning it into an outdoor breezeway. Clients may set the treatment room temperatures to suit themselves, select the music they prefer and even choose the color of LED light that washes over the wall of curtains. The intention is to give patrons the feeling of being completely removed from the hustle and bustle of the urban environment—and more in touch with nature.

In keeping with the goal to achieve the LEED certification, the project designers made use of local and regional materials, used FSC-certified and reclaimed wood, as well as rapidly renewable and recycled materials. 100% of the electric power comes from renewable energy-sources and the energy efficient lighting and the HVAC also save on energy. In keeping with the overall goal, the designers had all the graphics and printed materials produced in an environmentally friendly manner using post-consumer, chlorine-free paper with soy- and vegetable-based inks. This includes Nusta's cards, stationery, shopping bags, brochures and other promotional materials.

Design: Envision Design PLLC, Washington, DC
Project Team / Kendall P. Wilson, AIA, IIDA, LEED AP, Principal in Charge; Dawn Lovelace, LEED AP; Colleen Waguespack, IIDA, LEED AP; Brent Campbell, LEED AP
MEP Engineer / GHT Ltd.
Lighting Consultant / D.Gilmore, Lighting Design Inc.
Photography / Eric Laignel

ZOOTIQUE
Toronto Zoo, Toronto

The newly renovated 3000 sq.ft. Toronto Zoo retail shop, Zootique, was designed by David Milne of DMD Retail Design of Toronto. The store design builds on the sustainability values of the zoo by using everything from recycled paints to reconditioned materials in new and creative ways.

A giant banner in vibrant viridian green with the Zootique logo—accented with graphic representations of animal skin patterns—greets zoo visitors out front and invites them to look in through the wide expanses of glass storefronts. Inside, large graphic panels of the animal skin patterns float overhead, cover walls or create decorative friezes over the merchandised perimeter walls. The exterior banner and the interior signage and decorative panels are made of BIOflex vinyl, which is a strong biodegradable polymer fabric that is especially effective for OV, solvent or screen printing. It contains no toxic materials and is fade- and fungus-resistant.

Since this is actually a complete renovation of an existing store, elements of the previous shop have been reclaimed and reused. The original store fixtures were recycled and refurbished and finished in black. They

not only look brand new, but there was also a substantial cost saving to the client. "We though it was appropriate to use bamboo in several areas of Zootique, such as the main cash/checkout counters and the trim on the recycled gondola fixtures. The bamboo was not only fitting to use in a zoo environment because of its exotic look, but also because it is an environmentally sustainable product," said Phillip Yates of Geron & Associates, the distributoir of Plyboo Bamboo Products. Under the LEED rating system, Plyboo bamboo is eligible for credits. Even the paints were recycled. Steve Blasiak, a consultant with the company, says that Boomerang paints are composed of unused portions of recovered or reclaimed domestic paint remains, and contain very low VOC. The Boomerang Latex paints are approximately half the cost of regular latex paints. Also, Boomerang recycles 84% of everything it receives, including the metal containers.

The existing ballasts, wiring and conduit suspension were reused, but the inefficient incandescent downlights were replaced with compact fluorescents. Energy consumption was reduced as were the relamping and maintenance costs. Tomas Luknar of Edison Lighting said, "We increased the overall lighting levels and improved the quality of light with the merger of current technology and by reusing the main electrical components."

David Milne, president of the design firm said, "We did everything we could to make Zootique as environmentally sensitive as possible. With animal habitats around the world threatened by climate change and human impact, we felt it was essential to bring creativity and conservation together in this project." Shanna Young, executive director of marketing for the zoo agrees: "This redesign also aligns Zootique with the sustainability values that are at the center of what the zoo is all about."

Design / DMD Retail Design, Toronto—David Milne, President/Creative Director
Photography / Richard Johnson, www.richardjohnson.ca

The Great
ELEPHANT POO POO PA
COMPANY LIMITED™

ON CORPORATE SOCIAL RESPONSIBILITY

HELMEUT NEHER of UMDASCH

Based on values of the Umdasch Shopfitting Group and Umdasch Shop Concept company with its history and tradition going back over 140 years, Helmut Neher, the company's executive director said, "On the subject of Corporate Social Responsibility (CSR), we are on the right track as regards sustainability. CSR has become an essential trend concept which has even acquired a new dimension as a result of the crisis and the associated changes in values. The term 'sustainability' has been borrowed from forestry and describes the use of a renewable system that can be retained in its essential characteristics and that can be renewed in a natural way."

"There has been a noticeable change in values within the consumer sector. Organic products have long since established themselves in the social mainstream. LOHAS (Lifestyle of Health and Sustainability) has developed from a niche movement into a broad consumer trend. Most experts are convinced that this trend will not be diminished in times of economic difficulty, but rather that it will continue to grow. People increasingly want to know under what conditions the products they have purchased were manufactured and what influence it has on the environment. 'Trust' becomes a key in dealing with each other. That is why sustainable activity is not merely a sign of an ethical attitude but increasingly a precondition for sustained competitiveness."

After listing several world-famous brands, several of whose stores appear in this book and who demonstrate this trend, Neher continues with, "In the retail sector, the subject of sustainability extends far beyond the products on offer. The investment in the shops and the way they are operated is equally important. Even the (store) branding of the brand or shop in question should—indeed must—contain coherent statements on the subject of sustainability." Thus, as designers and manufacturers of fixtures and fittings, they are partners in the retail sector and must accept this challenge.

"In order to reconcile the high degree of individuality required of our customer projects with the basic need to make careful use of the available resources, when it comes to waste products, we follow the principle of 'avoidance comes before recycling which comes before disposal.' Unavoidable wood trimmings are not disposed of but are transferred via a pipeline to the communal heating power station next door, where they are transformed into CO_2-neutral energy. 'Green' power and heat are fed into the public network via a district heating pipeline and used to heat company and public buildings and private homes. In summer, heat-extraction machines use excess heat to cool the buildings."

Neher concludes with, "Within the Umdasch Shopfitting Group and Umdasch Shop-Concept Corporate Social Responsibility (CSR) is firmly anchored in the company's corporate strategy. We recognize our growing responsibility to protect the environment and to make sparing use of all the resources which we have at our disposal."

Markets + Specialty Foods + Dining Spaces

WHOLE FOODS MARKET
Bayhill, FL

Whole Foods, a national chain of natural and organic food markets, has been devoted to developing and using alternative energy and renewable energy sources in its markets. The company recently placed #1 on the U.S. Environmental Protection Agency's Green Power Partnership list, which means Whole Foods purchases green power for its stores to reduce the environmental impacts of the use of conventional electricity. Though the two stores shown here were not necessarily designed to be LEED accredited, they are the latest in the Whole Foods crop of green stores and do combine sustainable and recycled materials with many energy-saving technologies in their construction and design.

The Bayhill store was designed by Barron Schimberg and the Schimberg Group of Sarasota, FL. What makes it noteworthy—as well as the Naples store that follows this project—is that in addition to following the green/sustainable/energy-saving tenets of the Whole Foods Company, they are site-specific. These two stores were designed to fit in with the communities in which they are situated— to become part of a neighborhood and to be reflective of their shoppers and their lifestyles.

The inspiration for the Bayhill store was the client's fondness for a local restaurant that incorporates '50s-style modern straight lines offset and complemented by natural materials. Also, Schimberg notes, "Since the store is located near Disney World, we wanted to incorporate the ideals of Walt Disney—without the kitsch of Walt Disney." There are subtle touches that serve as an homage to Disney World, like the large circular soffits that provide signage opportunities and highlight three corners of the store. This concept can be found in all Disney's parks; the Epcot ball, the Castles in Magic Kingdom and the Tree of Life in Animal Kingdom. In addition to the decoration and signage opportunities, these curved elements provide vantage points to help shoppers orient themselves in the 52,000 sq.ft. space.

In addition to the highly decorative styling of the store, the Schimberg Group's design team followed Whole Foods' mission statement to "design and build all stores as environmentally friendly, responsibly and sustainably as possible." To that effort, north-facing clerestory windows and numerous skylights were included throughout the structure to allow for maximum daylight and to minimize the use of artificial light during the day. When the lighting is used, the highly efficient lighting plan includes ceramic metal halide lamps as well as T-5 and T-8 fluorescent lamps. By minimizing the bulb sources and types, maintenance is simpler and energy is saved. Energy is also economized by the use of a Glycol refrigeration system, which reduces the need for refrigerants, and a highly efficient mechanical system that incorporates outside air, high filtration and high SEER ratings. From the decorative standpoint, the designers specified and utilized recycled products, wheat board and other renewable materials, along with low VOC paints for the colorful artwork and the interior walls in the store.

Architect & Design / The Schimberg Group, Sarasota, FL—Barron Schimberg, AIA LEED AP; Principal
Décor & Signage / Studio Image, Inc. Austin, TX
Contractor / McIntyre Elwell &Strammer
Mechanical Engineer / Gramlich & Associates
Electrical Engineer / Harold Hart & Associates
Refrigeration Engineer / OchsnerEFS, p.c.
Photography / The Greg Wilson Group, Sarasota, FL

WHOLE FOODS MARKET
Naples, FL

According to Barron Schimberg of The Schimberg Group of Sarasota, FL, the architects and designers of the Whole Foods Market in Naples, FL. "incorporated elements taken from the natural beauty of Naples—with the local 'beachy' feel to create a highly sophisticated interior for this high-end tourist town." The design of this market, as well as others in the chain, is influenced by a Feng Shui master, who was consulted on the colors, the materials and the shapes that were to be used in the ultimate design. The design team at The Schimberg Group combined those recommendations with the eco-friendly mission of Whole Foods to create a green and sustainable store design.

"We used familiar wavy shapes, reminiscent of the beach and natural bright colors. The curve is the most dominant feature throughout—used both vertically and horizontally," says Schimberg. The curvature is evident in the serpentine soffits that swirl around the perimeter walls and serve as directionals for shoppers. That shape is again accentuated in the wood-laid floor of the café. The rounded floating discs that appear out in the 52,000 sq.ft. market highlight the islands

set out on the concrete floor. The concrete flooring was used to minimize off-gassing, as well as for the ease of maintenance. The hanging amoeba-shaped forms also carry some of the lighting used to accentuate the products on display below as shown in the produce area. The suspended boat-like "trellises" used to distinguish the check-out stations are reminiscent of the boating community that Naples is and historically has been.

Here, as in the Bayhill store, there are numerous windows and skylights designed to take advantage of the natural daylight. The lighting scheme, when in use, includes ceramic metal halides and T-5 and 8 fluorescent lamps. All efforts were made to save on energy use through efficient lighting and refrigeration technology and systems. Also, as stated in the previous project, the color-filled decoratives

and signage panels utilized recycled products, wheat board, renewable materials and low VOC paints.

One of the major attractions in the Naples market is the Lifestyle Café. In addition to its wood-covered floor and coffered ceiling, it is also furnished with an area of comfortable lounge chairs for those shoppers who would like a few moments off their aching feet or to visit with friends. Nearby are the Mediterranean-inspired restrooms that blend contemporary materials with familiar old world style architectural interiors—commonly found in Naples high-end residential homes. Materials that were used on the building interior reappear within to gain a continuity of texture.

Schimberg said, "The greening of these stores was accomplished by the entire team committing to the mission statement of the client, incorporating sustainable materials, efficient systems and collaborating with the team of experts. I believe stores, spaces, buildings can be designed as "green" as anyone wants, but if the process of that design is not collaborative in nature and includes the ideas and input from all team members, then the built-in efficiencies of that process are lost and create a less sustainable, less responsible project than if handled collaboratively. The end result of a collaborative effort is a more successful and 'green' project."

This project, like the Bayhill store, succeeds in being the result of the collaborative "greening" process and it also provides the community with a place that says—"I belong here and you are welcome."

Architecture & Design / The Schimberg Group,
Sarasota, FL—Barron Schimberg, AIA LEED AP,
Principal
Decor & Signage / Studio Image Inc., Austin TX
Contractor: McIntyre Elwell & Strammer
Mechanical, Electrical, Plumbing, Refrigeration
Engineer / Clive Samuels & Associates
Photography / The Greg Wilson Group, Sarasota, FL

I t's not easy being green—but being green might just make all the difference. Built from the ground up with a commitment to the environment around it, our store is our road map. From building with environmentally responsible materials and revitalizing the downtown district to using water wisely, reducing energy and waste, it's where we're going, and we hope you'll come along for the ride." That invitation appeared on the Hannaford Supermarket website to introduce the public to the company's new, LEED Platinum-certified 50,000 sq. ft. store in Augusta, ME. "In building our store, we recycled and reused most of the Cory High School building—walls, desks and all—that stood on this very spot for years." 96% of demolition debris and 99% of the contents of the building were either recycled or reused.

Hannaford Supermarkets invited Fore Solutions of Portland, ME, under the direction of Gunnar Hubbard, to serve as the green building and LEED consultant project manager. Together with a large number of consultants drawn from across the U.S. and Germany, a design and construction scheme was developed. Hubbard said, "Our goal was to ensure that LEED Platinum certification was the result of good integrated design, sound construction processes and reduced operating

FRESH CATCH

expenses to exemplify the long-term environmental commitment of Hannaford."

The first and most noticeable element in the market's design is the light. The space is flooded with natural daylight that streams in through the skylights, the clerestory windows and the numerous glazed openings to fill the atrium and the assorted areas within. Solar tubes add to the illumination, along with the energy-saving fluorescent lamps when needed. "Natural light is a beautiful thing, so we use it six different ways to illuminate our stores. It also feeds our photovoltaic panels, the largest installation in Maine, helping us to cut our power by almost half that of an average supermarket."

According to Michael Norton, in charge of communications for HBC (Hannaford Brothers

Mom was right – leaving the refrigerator door open wastes energy. (Are you trying to cool off all outdoors?) Our doors keep the heat out, the cold in - and energy costs down.

Corp.—owners of the supermarket chain), the store interior is "bright—clean—simple. The décor is similar to all Hannaford stores in striving for a bright, clean look. We try to minimize the number of signs and most of our signs are made with recycled materials. The décor also is influenced by the number of local and regional materials—and the highly renewable materials chosen for the project." An example is the Dakota Burl that was used in the pharmacy area and the customer service desk. It is a composite that looks like wood but actually is made of highly renewable agricultural products like straw and sunflower seeds—and that emits no VOCs. The concrete

floor—a regional material—is also durable for our highly trafficked store."

In addition to the above green and sustainable practices and materials, 70% of the wood used is FSC-certified and the 7000 sq.ft. green roof reduces water run-off and not only helps to insulate the store but also reclaims greenspace. Other water-saving devices and equipment have also been installed, including the iceless cases in the seafood area. Two geothermal wells, 750 feet below ground, help to regulate the store's interior temperature.

In the Hannaford website posting of its LEED certification, it said, "In planning our store, we weighed the materials at hand and chose the best solutions, trying to minimize our impact on the environment at the same time. (Our store)—it's big! It's new! It's kind of funky looking, but at its heart, our store is a neighborhood market. We chose the downtown location to attract more shoppers, and to make it easy to walk to, bike or bus to. And with lots of great programs (especially on green education and recycling) and partners, we think it's easier for us to reach the community if we're a part of the community."

More LEED-certified Hannaford stores are in the future for other Maine communities as well.

Green Building, LEED Consultant / Fore Solutions, Portland, ME—Gunnar Hubbard, Principal; Allison Zuchman, Project Manager
Architecture, Engineering / WBRC Architects/ Engineers, Bangor, ME
Design Architect / Next Phase Studios, Boston, MA—Rick Ames, Principal
Day lighting Consultant / Clanton & Assoc., Boulder, CO
Energy & Systems Design Engineering / Transsolar, Stuttgart, Germany
For Hannaford Bros Corp. / Fred Conlogue, Director Design Services; Rande Gray, Design Project Manager; Harrison Horning, Director Energy & Facility Management
Photography / Allison Zuchman, Fore Solutions & Courtesy of Hannaford Markets

CUB FOODS
Phalen, St. Paul, MN.

The Cub Foods supermarket that opened in the Phalen district of St. Paul, MN, is the first grocery store in Minnesota to achieve LEED Gold certification. According to Bryan Slattery, DSG's lead architect, "The challenge for us as a design team was to deliver to Cub the most energy-efficient store to date. We had to significantly reduce our typical carbon footprint, while keeping the Cub brand intact from an aesthetic and operational standpoint, and to do all this in the most cost-efficient manner possible."

Cub Foods, part of the Supervalu group of grocery stores, prides itself on its environmental philosophy: "We have a responsibility to minimize our environmental footprint and are committed to honoring our pledge as environmental stewards." Cub Foods was established in 1968 and has been providing its shoppers with the freshest foods and widest selection, as well as serving innovative, natural, ethnic and organic foods. Also, for many years the company has been involved in plastic-bag recycling and in a fresh-food "rescue plan" where perishable items that would otherwise be wasted are collected and donated to local food charities. As part of the GreenChill Advanced Refrigeration Partnership, Cub Foods uses only non-ozone depleting refrigerants in

all the refrigerated cases. "All of our business units and operation teams consistently work to identify and support business initiatives that are environmentally-friendly, ranging from promoting customer involvement in the company's recycling programs to further reducing energy usage in our stores and offices."

Forty-four skylights fill the ceiling of the new 62,900 sq.ft. store and using a solar-powered GPS system that tracks and redirects sunlight as needed, 75% of the regularly occupied spaces are illuminated. The lighting in the store is now more efficient than it has been in any previous Cub store. More energy has been saved through the use of LED lighting in the parking lot. The polished concrete floors eliminate the use of wax and stripping chemicals and thus reduces adding any hazardous fumes to the environment. 20% recycled or recyclable materials went into the building construction and half the waste from the tearing down of an existing structure was reused in the new building—or recycled. 75% of the new construction waste was recycled or converted into reusable materials.

This space has earned high commendations from St. Paul mayor, Chris Coleman, who said, "This store shows that small

Over 30 Varieties
of Fresh Herbs

Conventionally and
Organically Grown

investments can be good for neighborhoods, good for the environment, and good for the company's bottom line." Jamie Pfuhl, president of the Minnesota's Grocer's Association added, "The commitment Cub is making to the long-term well being of the environment, their customers and employees truly exemplifies what our hometown groceries are all about." The enthusiastic response from Cub shoppers to the new, bright, clean and clearly signed and defined store garnered this response from Mark Halverson, store director of Phalen Cub Foods, "We enjoy giving back to the community and now we are also giving back to the environment." In addition to the LEED certification, this store was also given Gold-level certification from the Environmental Protection Agency's GreenChill Partnership.

Design / DSG (Design Services Group), Eden Prairie, MN—Bryan Slattery, DSG lead architect
Photography / Courtesy of Supervalu

ISLAND GOURMET MARKET
Queen's Marketplace, Waikoloa. Hawaii

Though the team at A.D.M. Retail Planning & Architecture of Honolulu was not specifically designing for LEED certification, its new Island Gourmet Market certainly scored some high marks on the LEED chart. This 25,000 sq.ft. market is located in the Queen's Marketplace on the island of Waikoloa. According to Grant Sumile, the design principal, "the new concept market blends the best elements of a supermarket, gourmet market and convenience shopping to give customers a new and fresh way to receive great variety, great service and the best selection and ease of shopping in an upscale, homey-feeling environment." And—a green, eco-friendly environment at that!

In order to make shopping this market easy and convenient for the shopper, "the design response was to create a high, central ceiling space with varied architectural elements around the perimeter, creating different 'rooms' that coincided and highlighted the different merchandise departments." These different "rooms" are organized around the central dropped ceiling. Various tones of natural, sustainable woods are used and they are complemented by a mix of natural

and vibrant colors, graphic wall coverings, and backlit decorative acrylics "to create an inviting space that feels upscale, exciting and expresses a sense of Hawaii."

A photovoltaic lighting system was installed, and while most of the lighting is fluorescent, high-bay metal halide lamps were used for the general illumination—to allow for greater spacing and a lower quality of light fixtures. With the different light levels, the designers created depth and a sense of drama within the market. One of the unique features in the market is the Aloha Wine Bar, where customers can sit and sample the wines on sale in the market. The wood "waves" that separate the bar from the market are a combination of cherry wood and black-stained woods, and they blend elements of wine barrels, trellises and waves. Eco-friendly leather seating, accents of rouge and LEED-certified materials such as the Amtico architectural

flooring all add up to interest and sparkle and create a romantic atmosphere.

In addition to the floor tiles, which are composed of 40% pre-consumer recycled content and are GreenGuard Indoor Air Certified and use low-emitting adhesives or sealants, the acrylics from 3 Form also contain high levels of recycled content and low emitting materials. The paints (Wolf Gordon Scrub-Master) are all Green Seal compliant. They are water-based and formulated to ensure low

VOC content as set forth by the LEED Green Building rating system. The paints also contain no harmful chemical compounds.

Thus, adding these LEED accredited materials to the energy-saving lighting plan and the other recyclable materials used in the design and construction, the Island Gourmet Market makes a green statement amid the glorious greenery of the Hawaiian Islands—and has become a quaint, chic and cool destination for visitors and locals alike.

Architect, Designer / A.D.M. Retail Planning & Architecture, Honolulu, HI—Darin M. Fukunaga, Principal; Grant S. Sumile, AIA, Design Principal; Lian M. Nakaishi, Project Designer; Christina Pang-Capello, Interior Designer
Photography / Andrea Brizzi

The Greeks may have had a word for it—but so do the Finns. It is "vihrea" in Finnish and as evidenced by the look and feel of the Ruohonjuuri store, it obviously means "green." This "ekomarkt" or eco-market is described by Susanne Markkanen in her book "Shopping in Finland" as a store in which "ethics and ecological awareness are the guiding values—values which are reflected in both the wide range of environmentally friendly, organic products and in the atmosphere of the store itself."

Visually, the store is a symphony of shades and tints of green complemented by the off-white floors and ceilings. Arto Ranta-aho, the managing director of the company, says that the green color represents—"growth, reliability, trustworthiness—gives hope and is derived from nature. It is the color of Mother Earth." The mid-floor units are a clear, bright green relieved by a pattern of white leaves—the same pattern that appears in green to frame the wide windows that give shoppers

a clear view into the spacious store. Under a frieze of assorted green foods, shoppers find organically grown fruits and vegetables while jars, tins and boxes of other organic or natural foods are lined up on shelves of natural pine wood or in display cabinets of reclaimed materials. There are also items for the home, the bath, as well as toiletries, cosmetics and other locally produced craft items and fair and equitable trade items. Shoppers are encouraged to bring their own containers to refill with soaps, shampoos and detergents and other eco-friendly liquids that are on tap. Shoppers who bring their own bags to carry their purchases in are rewarded with some savings.

Finding one's way around the store and getting to know what is where is simplified by the black reused slate signs that appear either above eye-level as directionals or locators or at eye level on counters or in display arrangements to provide green information. Occasional live plants add to the green feel of the space and the energy-efficient lighting

provides a fresh, easy look at the shop and the product presentation.

As much as possible, the designers have used locally produced and available materials to construct and furnish the eco-market and recycled items for displayers. As Ranta-aho explains, "The floors are stone, the walls a combination of concrete and wood, and the ceilings are mainly concrete. The materials are easy to wash, maintain and they are durable." The Finnish pine wood and the units produced are by a local furniture company. The decorative display boxes, risers and cabinets were created from old wine, fruit and grocery boxes. Old storage package material has been reclaimed to create some

of the display walls. Old blackboards were salvaged, recycled and used for the previously mentioned signage. "These signs are ecological and durable in multiple uses. This also minimizes the use of paper for signs and such," says Ranta-aho. In addition, all textiles are recycled cotton or hemp. Environmentally certified carpets are used to highlight some areas—like the children's play space—while the lamps that are used to illuminate the store go with the other electrical appliances, like the freezer and refrigeration units, to conserve energy.

There are now several Ruohonjuuri stores in Finland and all are near or in shopping centers. All are easily accessible by public transport or by bicycle or by foot—and "other ecological means of transportation." The eco markets range in space from 3500 to 5500 sq.ft. and the ecoshops are about 2000 to 2500 sq.ft. in size. Shown here is the newest eco market that recently opened in East Helsinki.

Design Concept / MOZO, Helsinki—Anna Hamalainen, Concept Designer; Antti Vlisassi & Petri Rantonen, Designers; Susanne Markkanen, Retail Trend Specialist; Mats Langskog, Product Development Engineer; Annika Jarvelin, Graphic Designer
Photography / Courtesy of Mozo

P.O.D. (PROVISIONS ON DEMAND)
Brandies University, Waltham, MA

P.O.D. (Provisions on Demand) is a new concept—for a new generation—and done in a new eco-friendly, green/sustainable way. The design project, by Miller Zell of Atlanta, GA, offers a convenience store with a twist for the Aramark Group that provides food services on campuses across the U.S. P.O.D. not only provides frozen-meal options, chilled beverages, snacks and "everyday essentials," but also offers an on-campus source for healthy options such as fresh fruits, sushi, low-carb and gluten-free selections, hot sandwiches and fair-trade coffee.

With today's Gen Y college student as the target market and his/her desire for a healthy lifestyle, environmental responsibility, and selection and choice at fair prices, the 2800 sq.ft. space in Brandies University in Waltham, MA, serves it all up in a green/sustainably designed ambience. The design reinvents the campus experience by blending corner store quick convenience with modern market style.

According to the Miller Zell design team, "The P.O.D. vibe conveys a modern market style with graphic simplicity, a sophisticated palette and a sense of humor." A signature focal point is the mural based on archival photography of the Waltham campus. It has become a source of pride for each school (serviced by Aramark with a P.O.D.) to find

[HOT] **RECHARGE** [COLD]

FRESH BREWED COFFEE • FOUNTAIN DRINKS

the more eccentric photos from their past and feature one as a major design element. The space is illuminated with energy-efficient indirect fluorescent lighting to affect a soft, inviting ambiance, and wall washers enhance the perimeter and accentuate the graphics. The overhead ceiling clouds, constructed of lightweight wood and low-emitting composite material, add to the comfort level. The modular components, created and installed by Miller Zell, seem to make the allotted space appear more spacious. Recyclable materials were used for the shelving and the millwork was delivered from within 200 miles of the site, thus reducing delivery-related gasoline emissions. The Centiva flooring, fabricated domestically, contains recycled materials

and existing doors have been reused as well. As for the equipment in this P.O.D., 90% of the Energy Star-eligible equipment is Energy Star-rated, as are all the light fixtures for high efficiency and low voltage. In keeping with the green attitude, paints, coatings and the laminate adhesives are all low emitting products. The cast stone panels and wood flooring are also cost-effective materials that provide a residential finish that is not usually associated with convenience stores.

P.O.D. "creates a hip yet practical pit stop for the time-pressed undergrad by offering an abundance of healthy selections and everyday essentials equal to those found in off-campus stores." This store is also eco-friendly, green and sustainable.

Retail Design & Store Planning, Shopfitting / Lighting / Juno Lighting Inc., Des Plaines , IL Photography / Courtesy of Miller Zell, Atlanta, GA

The award-winning and LEED Gold certified Founding Farmers restaurant was designed to the owners' specifications: low energy output, renewable materials, and a fun, casual environment. This 8500 sq.ft., two-level dining experience located just three streets away from the White House in Washington, DC, is the project of the North Dakota Farmer's Union (NDFU) and they wanted the restaurant to "recognize the importance of agriculture and farming in America while establishing itself as an organization concerned with sustainable and well-thought-out design." Also, the design intent, according to the design team of Core Architects of Washington, DC, was "to put a twist on the classic farm."

"The materials used are what you would commonly find in a farmhouse: wood beams, white-washed barn wood and standing seam metal. We've used them in ways not originally intended, creating more interest. We've also taken classic architectural forms you'd see on a farm and abstracted them, such as the façade of the house you enter and the silo-inspired booths you sit in within," explained the designers. Local artisans, like artist Tom Ruttkay, were commissioned to add to the new/old ambiance while also underscoring the "mission of the restaurant."

Dining at Founding Farmers is a warm, friendly farm-house experience. Much of the natural light that fills the restaurant comes through the glazed façade, which also presents the centrally located stairway that connects the two levels and the bar on the right. An illuminated case filled with glass jars of preserved fruits and vegetables sets the tone for the theme. The reclaimed wood beams overhead complement the pine wood floors. Long, handcrafted community tables are welcoming and family-friendly, while the semi-circular, silo-inspired booths provide more intimacy. A modicum of privacy, between the booths, is provided by the green sprouting acrylic screens, which are made of

40% post-industrial recycled resin. Dropped wagon-wheel-like elements are suspended over the semi-circular booths—reiterating the shape—while in other areas wagon-wheel-inspired lighting fixtures add to the farmhouse feeling. Some of the walls are sheathed in white-washed barn wood with an occasional barn red door serving as an accent and a complement to the matte gray finish of the standing seam metal walls.

The pine flooring was reclaimed from a barn in West Virginia and the brick that is on some walls is also reclaimed, from Vintage Brick Salvage. The carpet, by Blueridge, was certified by Scientific Certification Systems as an "environmentally preferable product." The wood used for the furniture and furnishings was harvested from forests in Pennsylvania and manufactured in North Carolina—"all within 500 miles of the job site." Half of all of the materials used were manufactured within that 500-mile radius. Also adding points toward LEED certification was the fact that more than 15% of the material was reclaimed. Duraprene, which is composed of wood pulp from sustainably managed forests, post-industrial waste, and recycled post-consumer waste was used for the graphic wall coverings and low VOC paints, coatings and varnishes also earned points for the "indoor environmental quality." Also contributing to the certification was the higher efficiency HVAC system, the Energy Star-rated equipment and the water-saving devices that were used.

The philosophy of Founding Farmers is "to operate, serve and live green in the heart of the American family farmer" and as the team at Core Architects adds—"Family Farmers is here to bring you the bounty of the true farm-to-table choices in an environment dedicated to sustainability."

Architect & Designer / CORE ARCHITECTURE, Washington, DC—Peter F. Haystak III, AIA, IIDA, Designer, Architect; Deborah Lerner LEED AP, Project Manager; Allison Cooke LERED AP, Designer; Danny Chapman LEEDAP, Intern
MEP Engineers / FACE Associates
Lighting Designer / MCLA
Graphic Designer, Signage / Allison Seth , Seth Design Group
Photography / Michael Moran Photography, NY

The Pizza Fusion restaurant in Palm Beach Gardens, FL, was the first pizzeria to be LEED certified—and Gold certified at that! According to Mike Gordon, VP of store development and co-founder of Pizza Fusion, "This certification represents our commitment to building all our restaurants to this standard." Pizza Fusion specializes in a full-service approach to gourmet pizzas, focaccio sandwiches, salads and desserts—all in "their purest form"—organic and "untainted by artificial additives in chic dining destinations." As the company proclaims on its website, "Pizza Fusion is pioneering the organic and environmental restaurant movement as the most eco-friendly restaurant in America."

Staying true to the company's motto— "Saving the Earth One Pizza at a Time"—the restaurant, as shown here, was designed with a socially conscious approach and used LEED standards for the selection of the materials and furnishings. The eco elements include countertops made of recycled glass bottles collected from other Pizza Fusion restaurants and "manufactured using a cradle-to-cradle approach," bamboo flooring, 30% recaptured industrial concrete, non VOC paints, adhesives and finishes, Energy Star-certified appliances, insulation from recycled blue jeans, recycled composite boards used for the ceiling

baffles, low-voltage and low-heat lighting and furniture made from reclaimed wood. Even the toilet paper is 100% post-consumer recycled.

The building's architecture fits in comfortably with its Florida location and the large windows allow daylight to enter into the dining area. Adding to the "fresh-organic" and eco-friendly ambiance, while providing reading material to those waiting to place their orders, is the story book wall. It is a collage of copy and images that underscores the company's commitment to being eco-friendly. The well-illuminated service counter is backed up by a "green grass wall" that is recycled plastic material. The dividing partition between the counter and the seating is a checkerboard of shadow boxes filled with either ecological messages or retail items with the Fusion Pizza logo. The logo—a big red tomato—appears on the floor mat and as appliqués on walls and the divider. It provides not only accents of bright color, but messages such as that it's

okay to throw away the plastic cutlery and the salad containers because they are 100% biodegradable. Red appears on the seats in the dining area, adding a warm, rich accent to the otherwise neutral, natural color scheme. Some of the furniture was salvaged, recycled or reclaimed from local sites. The company's eco-friendly standards extend to its delivery service, where its biodegradable and recycled cardboard boxes are delivered in company-owned hybrid, energy-saving automobiles.

In commending Pizza Fusion on attaining its LEED Gold certification, Rick Fedrizzi,

CEO and founding chair of U.S.Green Building Council said, "Pizza Fusion has demonstrated a strong commitment to the environment and by achieving certification they also demonstrate a commitment to the health, comfort and well-being of their customers and employees."

Interior Design / Casa Conde—Cesar Conde
Architecture & LEED Certification / Square One Architecture—John Garra
Photography / Mike Butler Photography, Coral Gables, FL

I t has been called "The greenest restaurant in the Bay area" and with three locations in San Francisco and more being built, Mixt Greens is not only spreading the gospel of "green eating" but of green retail design. Leslie Silverglide, one of the restaurant partners, explained in an interview for *EcoAsia* magazine, that Mixt Greens was created " to serve delicious gourmet and healthy meals and build a business with an environmentally sustainable core. Every aspect of our operation minimizes our environmental impact and we strive to be a leader and model for other businesses." The simple, minimalist and very eco-friendly design "showcases the complementary nature of responsible architecture and progressive restaurant practices," according to William Duff of William Duff Architects, designer of the space.

From the numerous, very large and lightly tinted windows that allow the daylight in but keep down the solar heat, the raw existing

ceiling, and down to the eco-timber, Forest Stewardship—approved wood floor—it is all green. The bench that wraps around the perimeter and under the windows, the front of the counter and the drink and waste stands are all constructed of Kirei board: reclaimed agricultural fiber that is pressed with non-toxic adhesives. It is a product of the rapidly renewable sorghum plant. According to Duff, "it is both sustainable and rich in visual interest, with strong horizontal banding and a deep natural color." The table tops used with the benches are topped with 100% recycled detergent bottles. The focal point of the restaurant is the long transaction counter where customers line up and where the salad options are on display. The counter top is made of locally harvested slate that adds

another dark accent to the design scheme. A signature element of the design is the sculptured, C-shaped element that anchors the end of the counter in which glass shelves provide an opportunity to display merchandise. The tall, rectangular wall decoration is a 3 form ecoresin panel that incorporates 40% post-industrial regrind content.

Along with the use of all FSC-certified woods and the formaldehyde-free plywood, zero VOC paints were used throughout and 100% recycled paints were used for the dark colors. The architects/designers also considered the use of energy and installed a dual-zone HVAC system with temperature and ventilation controls. Compact fluorescent lamps, on timers and sensors, are used for optimal energy performance lighting and the refrigeration equipment is also Energy Star-rated.

A visit to the Mixt Greens website introduces a company that flaunts its greenness. Among their highlighted items are the company's pride in its sustainable food, the green restaurant settings, its compliance with compostable packaging and green cleaning. The company mitigates its carbon emissions by purchasing renewable energy credits through Renewable Choice and much of that comes from wind power. "Our mission is to introduce and enable customers to experience fresh, quality, organic, local and seasonal ingredients offered as innovative gourmet meals while maintaining the company's environmental ethic.".

Design / William Duff Architects, San Francisco, CA—William S. Duff Jr., AIA, LEED AP; Amelia Dolan; Alison White; Sheryl Fetterly
Photographer / JD Peterson

For the past five years Zoffoli Architecture of Santiago has been designing and building Sushi House restaurants in Chile. Inspired by Japanese architecture and design and its use of natural materials, this 2100 sq.ft. space is the latest in the chain. It not only achieves the desired Japanese atmosphere, but it is also eco-friendly in the selection and use of materials and energy conservation.

Alessandro Zoffoli, the architect, said, "We have evolved this concept and have been inspired in the use of ecological material such as is used in Japanese architecture." Bamboo is featured in its many forms and sizes—from finger width to several inches in diameter to tall rods that set the scene in the open windows or form a decorative, eye-catching frieze over the open-to-viewing sushi prep area. Smaller bamboo rods are tightly arranged in decorative geometric patterns set into the black lacquered screen near the entry into the restaurant. They are also used to line the wall behind the hostess' reception desk. Adding

to the geometric design of the space is the bold swath of bamboo stalks lined up on the ceiling to dramatically highlight the seating area. The band descends on the far wall to accentuate that location. Reclaimed wood is used to frame and face the prep area. "It highlights the action and adds some warmth to the serene, neutral and natural scene."

The stones that become decorative elements on the light cream-colored walls were found on the ground of the construction site, and natural stone tiles are used as flooring material. As Zoffoli reiterates, "The materials that were used are not harmful to nature, as they are reused or reclaimed woods, stone tiles and bamboo which replenishes itself quickly." In order to be more energy efficient and economize on power consumption, fluorescent lamps are used in the recessed ceiling fixtures for general lighting and low-voltage metal halide lamps serve for accent illumination. "The idea was to create a peaceful and balanced place to eat that exudes a sense of freshness and simplicity in which the use of natural materials makes this a green project."

Architecture, Design / Zoffoli Architecture, Santiago—Alessandro Zoffoli; Marcelo Lopez
Contractor / Zoff Ltd., Santiago
Photography / Marco Mendizabel

Jose Orrego Herrera, the architect/designer and principal at Metropolis in Lima, was asked to design a sustainable prototype design for the Altomayo Café Company that could be reproduced throughout Peru and possibly in some of its South American neighbors. Orrego found his inspiration for the design in the San Martin jungle, in the Amazon, where the coffee that plays such a major role in the café's menu comes from.

Orrego said, "In spite of the act of drinking coffee being an urban experience, an ethno-urban concept was crafted where the jungle sensation was incorporated into the city—creating a kind of oasis." Though most of the palette is natural and neutral, it is the giant green graphic wall—a jungle setting—that sets the scene, captures the mood and makes the strong visual impact. Panels of this "greening" also frame the entrance into the café. "The use of natural stones and wood helped us to create a natural ambiance and the graphics, used in a super scale, created the jungle sensation that makes the difference between many imported concepts that we find in our city and the Altomayo Cafe."

The design concept is also tied in naturally with the selection of sustainable materials. All stone applications, as in the major perimeter wall with the multi-TV monitor unit opposite the bar, are natural and have been recycled from left over pieces from a local quarry. The

flooring, also natural recycled stone, adds color and texture as well as a dimension to the setting. Readily renewable woods were used for the café furniture.

Herrera is, in many ways, ahead of the curve in introducing and using sustainable materials in his architecture and interior designs. He says, "All materials and furnishings were selected because they contain a high percentage of reused base materials." For the lighting in the café he specified energy-saving, high-efficiency lamps and LED lighting.

Architecture, Design / Metropolis, Lima—Jose Orrego Herrera, Principal and Creative Director
Photography / Courtesy of Metropolis

L'AMANTE—LOVE BIO BAR
Portogruaro, Venice, Italy

It is a return to nature—to the earth—to the simple things and the simple ways of doing things. As the design team of Costa Group of La Spezia sees it, "Today people want to eat healthy—enjoy natural foods—and gather in wholesome settings, close to nature. The Love Bio Bar is a green meadow."

L'Amante or Love Bio Bar is located in Portogruara, near Venice, and is as natural and eco-friendly as possible. The designers relied heavily on recycled and recyclable wood products, safe finishes and the reuse of materials. Thinly split logs of fallen trees are used to pattern one of the walls, while split logs of a readily renewable species of tree adds texture and pattern to another wall in the space. Chunks of logs serve as cocktail tables, stools and displayers and some of the very unique and distinctive chairs and tables are actually created out of roots of fallen trees—given a new existence and use in the Love Bio Bar. Natural and not chemically treated teak wood faces the main bar. Complementing the natural setting is the use of local stone.

In addition to some contemporary furniture, the designers added stall-like seating units fashioned from recycled wood where guests can sit and be part of the bar's action. This area is backed up with a wall of backlit recycled coffee cups. A giant graphic of luscious red lips appears on another wall and throughout the café the word "LOVE" appears over and over again.

Franco Costa, president of the design group, said, "The furnishings have to perform like an invisible butler: their only function is to emphasize the product displayed and to communicate and enhance its qualities. This happens more evidently in a shop where the real fulcrum is nature." Since the emphasis at Love Bio Bar is on natural and organic fruits and vegetables, all materials and colors are linked to the "natural theme" that the venue is based on. Natural paints and reclaimed and untreated timber add to the green design.

Design / Costa Group, Ricco del Golfo, La Spezia, Italy
Photography / Moreno Carisone, CostaGroup.net

CELLAR 360
Ghirardelli Sq. San Francisco, CA

Located in the historic Woolen Mill building in Ghirardelli Square—one of San Francisco's top tourist attractions—is the new/old Cellar 360. The Miroglio Architecture and Design firm of Oakland, CA, was challenged to create a prototype design in the 6000 sq.ft. space that would feature wine tasting, a small café/restaurant, retail wine sales and a wine and culinary education center complete with a demonstration kitchen. What makes Cellar 360 unique is that all the wine on display and available is obtained from 28 wineries around the world that are all controlled by Foster's Wine Estates.

Joel Miroglio, the architect/designer explains, "Given the multiple uses of the space and its limited size, we opened the entire floor up so that even though some spaces are physically and acoustically separate, they are all visibly accessible to customers. Because of the historic nature of the space, we preserved all the existing columns. The original six-inch-thick wood plank floor was also revealed and refurbished, as were the original brick walls. We chose to reuse the entire existing interior envelope of this warehouse space rather than build a new shell."

Upon entering Cellar 360, the 50-foot-long wine tasting bar, with its hand wrought zinc top, is the first feature viewed. Custom light fixtures, fashioned from recycled wine bottles, illuminate the bar and the custom tasting tables. These are converted from recycled redwood wine barrels. The chandeliers are constructed out of recycled staves of French oak wine barrels. Tying the whole space

together is a sinuous, wine bottle ceiling element that starts at the entry and snakes its way back using 2000 recycled wine bottles backlit with LED lighting. Further in the shop is the retail area, with its specially designed wine gondolas on caster wheels for greater flexibility in reconfiguring this area as needed. These fixtures show off some of the bottles as well as store stock below in closed storage cabinets. In the retail area, the shopper will find unique wine and food products, along with the numerous types of wines. The cherry wood and zinc-topped cash counter includes a feature display area.

There is both indoor and outdoor seating in the full-service, gourmet charcuterie restaurant, where the service kitchen also serves as the demonstration kitchen for specified

lectures or events. Due to the complexity of space, the design team added a wine concierge element in the center of the store. Here one can get answers to questions about the wines and the food. The overhead plasma video monitor features images of the Foster Wineries and footage from the demo kitchen during culinary events. The Cellar's instruction space includes seating and desks which can be arranged to suit the instruction being offered.

Summing up this project, Miroglio said, "This adaptive reuse strategy allowed us to effectively 'recycle' the entire space. The project also incorporates a new, high-efficiency air conditioning system—hidden within the recycled bottle ceiling spine element. The project materials include oak, cherry and recycled redwood and also steel, zinc and the existing brick walls. The overall design intent is that Cellar 360 will provide a unique and comprehensive wine experience which touches on all aspects of wine's relationship to contemporary living"—while being sustainable and eco-friendly.

Architecture, Design / Miroglio Architecture &
Design, Oakland, CA—Joel Miroglio
Assoc. Historic Architect / Architectural
Resources Group, San Francisco
Photography / David Wakely Photography, San
Francisco

MARQUES DE RESCAL WINERY STORE
El Ciego, Alava, Spain

In Spain, at this time, "green" means reuse, repurpose and recycle. For the retail store for the Marques de Riscal Winery in El Ciego, it meant, "recycling, rearranging and making the best use of existing furniture. In other words, the new shop design should bear the green philosophy—the optimum combination of new materials with existing furniture to effectively introduce the products and create a memorable shopping experience—at a reasonable price." That statement by Carlos Aires, principal and creative director of Marketing Jazz, a Madrid-based design firm, set the design concept shown here. The shop, in the winery, is located next to the area's great tourist attraction: the Frank Ghery-designed hotel in El Ciego—in Alava—in northern Spain.

In addition to the sale of the Marques de Riscal wines, the client wanted to use the shop to sell wine-related products. The brand name would serve as an umbrella for other products such as T-shirts, aprons and signature souvenirs, as well as cosmetics made from grapes, organic foods that go with wine, books and bar accessories. In describing how the store was laid out, Aires explained, "We organized the space based on

the location of the lamps (lighting fixtures) already in the store." Instead of the cash desk being up front, it was moved to the rear and in its place is a piece of furniture to welcome clients. A walkway was created to set off the central brown carpeted area and to distribute the cables and lights for the cash desk and each focal display unit. This walkway is lined with LED Neon-Flex lights to create a visual experience—to give the impression that the area was floating above the ground. Custom-crafted black pine wood tables were constructed and used to show off the wines and impulse items. These displayers or "stages" in "the theater of retailing" that Aires was creating—provide symmetry with the existing lighting fixtures. The truncated translucent lampshades make a strong statement in the space and the dark-stained wood display tables set directly under them are an inverted replica of the shape of these lampshades.

The windows in the left-hand perimeter wall were turned into merchandise "cupboards" and include not only images of the various wineries whose products are on sale here, but also some of the hanger-hung garments. Following the concept that in

most countries people move to the right, the right side of the space became the major focal merchandise display area. Existing wall shelves are now covered over with panels with cut-out openings. This now becomes a wall of shadow boxes illuminated with LEDs and energy-efficient fluorescents. Storage areas are provided in the cabinets below. "This is how we managed to individually display the best wines whilst hiding the stock stored below," Aires said. In Spain, pine wood is considered a sustainable material and was freely used in this design. The white panels are DM with a pine wood finish and acrylic and water based paints were used throughout.

The natural, neutral look of the space is enhanced by the old pine wood ceiling beams and trusses, along with the original stone work that add to the look and feel of the wine-making process. It is reuse and repurpose.

Design / Marketing Jazz, Madrid Spain—Carlos Aires, Creative Director
Photography / Luis Aires, Airephotostudio, Madrid

"BEING GREEN—IT'S NOT EASY"

DAVID WRIGHT of DALZIEL + POW

"Environmental sustainability, or 'The Green Issue,' is no longer a subject that we can avoid, or leave to others to sort out. All businesses, including design, need to tackle this head on and affect a change in their behavior. We are all asking how to approach this issue and the challenge to be 'greener.' We need to change how we interact with suppliers and clients and look to everything from our own in-house initiatives to the materials and finishes we specify for any design project.

   We need to accept that in the not-too-distant future, more robust, sustainable policies will be a requirement. Ethical issues go hand-in-hand with environmental issues and brands will be challenged on their practices. Recent research shows that 74% of UK citizens want more information on a company's social and ethical behavior. Think about Corporate Social Responsibility!

   We must embrace sustainability in a healthy way—try to integrate it into our business. Good business examples are on the increase: from brands who have always taken a sustainable position throughout their operation, to examples of established brands that are starting to make moves in the right direction. Design will have a dramatic impact on the environment. Think about all the printed materials we produce as graphic designers; where does the paper come from? Is the forest sustainable? What about the printing process and its waste? Let's look at the impact and usage of print, which is the UK's fifth-largest manufacturing industry. Two thousand trees are used to produce one day's circulation of a major UK tabloid newspaper—now consider that paper can be recycled up to six times and one ton of recycled paper saves 3.3 cubic yards of landfill—and seventeen trees. Interior designer specifications—a huge range of lighting, materials, fixtures and fittings—heavily influence our clients' build and running costs. We are all part of the problem, but as designers we are crucially positioned to make a difference. We are commited to working together with our clients and supply chains to deliver environmentally responsible design solutions, tackle issues at the creative stage and develop strategies for ongoing sustainability. We believe that this should be central to what we do and how we do it.

   We all have a responsibility to the environment. We need to be ahead of the game on this and—rather than being dragged along by the legislation—we must turn this into a positive, with increased profits through lower running costs and improved consumer perception of our activities and attitudes.

   Consumers are starting to demand nothing less.

From an inter-office paper prepared by David Wright, marketing director,
Dalziel +Pow Design Consultancy, London

Home Fashions + Exhibits + Displays

The Green Depot, located in a landmark 1885 building on NYC's rebounding Bowery is a "first" in several ways. It is the first of a nation-wide roll out by The Green Depot and the first LEED Platinum-certified retail space in NYC. Sarah Beatty, founder of The Green Depot, opened her first store in Brooklyn in 2005, but for this 6000 sq. ft. prototype she called upon Mapos, a NY based full architectural and design service headed by Colin Brice and Caleb Mulvena. The objective was to design a store that would not only be compatible with the venerable setting, but help explain and promote the use of the numerous green home supplies.

Mapos's designers restored the Queen Anne-style façade to its original glory, but they created a "dynamic, branded and modern interior," reported Mike Albo in *The New York Times*. "The smart green filter graphics and well-organized displays made the store feel like a child-friendly interactive wing of the

Bamboo
Paneling

Cellulose
Insulation

Eco-Resin
Panels

Engineered
Wood Flooring

Fiber Cement

Formaldehyde-
Free Insulation

FSC-Certified
Cedar Siding

FSC-Certified
Plywood

High-Efficiency
HVAC system

LED Lighting

Locally-
Fabricated
Light Shades

Low-VOC
Laminates

Low-VOC MDF

Low-VOC OSB

Mold-Resistant
& Recycled
Wallboard

Natural Cotton
Fiber Insulation

Natural
Linoleum Tile

Non-Toxic
Adhesives,
Caulks &
Sealants

LED Storefront
Signage

Reclaimed Oak

Reclaimed
Windows

Recycled
Glass &
Concrete
Countertops

Recycled
Glass Pavers

Recycled
Glass Tile

Recycled
Rubber
Roofing

Recycled
Steel Studs

Recycling
Systems

Refinished
Wood Flooring

Reused
"Found"
Objects

Solarban
Low-E Glass

Water
Reclamation
System

WaterSense
Certified
Plumbing

Museum of Natural History—in a good way. The whole place seems playful and educational and gave me that goofy I'm learning' feeling."

Mapos' team developed the palette of materials that would reflect the look of Green Depot by searching and selecting from the retailer's extensive selection of sustainable materials. The result shows that green can be new, fresh, colorful, warm and modern. In a way, inspired by artists that have in the past inhabited the space—a former YMCA building—the store is divided into a series of building slices to reveal the inner workings of sustainable architecture. Custom-designed sliding dividers and partitions are used to departmentalize the space. These dividers are made up of locally salvaged windows and window frames—selected and arranged by

Mapos. A locally fabricated, custom-designed "cloud" lamp shade that references the Green Depot's logo draws passers-by into the store. The antique brick walls and rehabbed wood floors are not only sustainabl" but they add to the inviting, friendly ambiance of the store.

A highly flexible fixturing system that combines recycled and repurposed fixtures from old and long-gone stores are refinished using low VOC paints and adhesives and recycled materials. The design of the bamboo and recycled glass design desk and the point-of-sales fixtures were inspired by the work of the Belgian artist Jan De Cock just as the previously mentioned "building slices" were inspired by Gordon Matta-Clark's work. A big attraction and draw up front is the wooden cleaning bar station that combines reclaimed bar fixtures with custom tap handles. This

area is an open invitation to the environmentally aware to refill their empty cleaning product bottles with Green Depot's proprietary cleaning liquids. Among the numerous unique areas and features that not only "show to sell" but "show to know" is the iconic paint wall—a color filled expanse of sample colors of Green Depot's low VOC paints, and the interactive light booth, where shoppers can compare the light output of various types of energy-efficient light bulbs. The store's own environmental lighting plan incorporates the latest in high-output fluorescent lighting, LED task lighting and CFL (compact fluorescent lighting) technology.

The resulting space, according to the designers, is "a hybrid of retail store and interactive educational center designed to empower the customer to make informed choices on sustainable building and lifestyle products."

Architecture + Design / Mapos, LLC, New York—Colin Brice; Caleb Mulvena
Photography / Dave Pinter

KEMNER HOME COMPANY
Bad Bederkesa, Niedersachsen, Germany

The Kemner Home Company has been providing home furnishings and home fashion accessories for over a century in Bad Bederkesa, near Hanover, in Germany. In keeping with the times and a desire to update and expand, the company called upon Wolfgang Gruschwitz of Gruschwitz GmbH of Grobenzell to convert the tired space into a "room" concept selling floor, where the focus would be on event shopping with theme settings and an open traffic pattern. Gruschwitz had to turn a space of over 51,000 sq.ft. into a series of easily seen, easily located and easily shopped zones, each highlighted with decorative and extensive graphics and signage. The space had to flow, and in addition, it had to be green, sustainable in its use of materials and also energy efficient.

Setting the "home" theme is the spacious, airy two-story atrium at the entrance, with a flowing fountain as its centerpiece. Pseudo rooftops of red clay tiles and semi-circular balconies with overhangs of terra-cotta tiles turn this enclosed space into an open courtyard. According to the designer, the circulating water has a cooling effect in the summer and in the winter it supplies a welcoming moisture to the air. Leading out from this courtyard are the entrances to the various departments of the store. According to Wolfgang Gruschwitz, "People liked it very much (the old concept) so our challenge was not to affront the people with a totally new design but to be so innovative that the old-fashioned style would disappear." "Emphasize your strengths" was the slogan for the new design concept: make those areas that were previously strong stronger—and larger with more effective presentation. In addition, the goals were to bring in a newer, younger clientele while making the new look acceptable to the older, more traditional customers—and be green.

Signage plays an important role in the

new concept. With the enlarged kitchen area and the rearrangement of the departments or zones in the vast space, the signage not only offers an overview of what is where, but also adds color and visual stimulation to the different areas. "With the new signage that is bigger, colorfully conceived and a combination of graphic images and letters, the results are extraordinary. The traditional customers are easily able to find the new locations," Gruschwitz says. Graphic images also play a vital part in this design concept. As Gruschwitz explains, "We combined big images and emotional signs—smaller elements to discover and larger ones to attract people to special areas—'crazy' or fanciful objects combined with 'normal' or usual objects to stop shoppers—intrigue them—get them thinking—like the whirlpool bath shown in a graphic forest setting surrounded by an assortment of beds."

Shoppers are led through the store by the carefully planned and executed lighting plan. Illuminating the various display and product areas had to be considered along with energy-saving efficiency. Warm daylight 35W metal halide lamps are used with filters and different types of reflectors, because of the light they produce and their cost and

energy-saving values. The accent lights are on timers and motion sensors appear in the display niches, storage rooms and lavatories. The mostly neutral color palette of beige and whites effectively serves as a setting for the color-filled product display. Most of the store's floors are covered with a beige carpet, though tile is used in the kitchen area. Some of the zones have open ceilings and the original wood-beam construction is visible, along with the insulation material. In others, decoratively finished gypsum ceilings delineate the areas or "rooms." Throughout, low-VOC paint finishes were used and some of the furniture has a natural finish. The flooring and wall covering materials are recyclable .

Going along with the greening, the Kemner Company has special events and conducts seminars on sustainability, energy-saving measures, renewable energy, solar collections and wind power.

Design / Gruschwitz GmbH, Grobenzell,
Germany—Wolfgang Gruschwitz, Principal/
Designer
Photography / Courtesy of Kemner Home Co.

ECO SHOPPE
Austin, TX

Kiku Obata, president of the design firm bearing her name, said, "By sharing knowledge, expertise and well-being, Eco Shoppe elevates green living beyond being just green to connect personally with how shoppers live, and their desire to create their own safe, healthy and nurturing lifestyle." The design team not only created the brand strategy for this new retail concept, but was also responsible for the store design and layout, custom fixture design, signage and graphics, and merchandise segmentation and strategy. In addition to all of the above, it was done with an environmentally responsible vision so as to receive LEED-CI certification for the project.

The 4400 sq. ft. store in "one destination delivers products, services and education for living an eco-friendly and healthy lifestyle," according to Steve Rolfes, director of the Eco

Shoppes. The space is easily shopped thanks to the graphic signage that identifies the various zones in the store: Purify & Renew, Create & Thrive, Care & Comfort, Enrich & Delight, and Learn & Discover. The color-keyed graphics/signage panels that stand out off the perimeter walls serve not only as focal elements but as unifying devices for the great variety of product-offer in each area. The reclaimed timber floor, the eco-friendly wood veneers on the walls and the light-colored tables and risers are all quite neutral and help to affect a pleasant flow through the space. Using custom designed fixtures that are versatile and adaptable, and the fresh clear colors, each zone has a personality of its own. The product signage panels explain the area's part in creating a healthier and more positive green home and life.

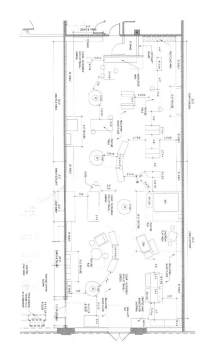

In designing a green space for green products, Obata and the design team specified rapidly renewable materials such as bamboo composite products and veneer. No protective surfaces were used on the interior signage, since the material options had unsustainable qualities. The fixtures for the store were produced by idX Corp. of St. Louis. This manufacturer of consumer environments claims that "sustainability is an inherent part of idX, from our own buildings and manufacturing processes to providing environmental sustainability services." The fixtures have 36% recycled content and all the composite wood products are FSC Certified with no added urea-formaldehyde. In addition, all glue and adhesives used are low VOC. idX also provided sustainability guidance to the design team with regard to HVAC, water, construction

waste and daylight use.

The green store carries numerous eco brands and all are selected for their green credentials, modern style and sense of design, and their unique benefit to everyday living. This prototype design, created for The Vitamin Shoppe Industries—the parent company—will be rolled out in other cities in the very near future.

Design / Kiku Obata, St. Louis, MO
Design Team / Kiku Obata; Farrah Katzer; David Leavey, AIA, LEED AP; Kristen Malone; Paul Scherfling; Todd Owyoung; Carole Jerome
Eco Shoppe / Roberta Modena
Fixtures / IDX Corp., St. Loius, Mo
Photography / Jon Miller. Hedrich Blessing Photography, Chicago, IL

GREEN HOME CHICAGO (GHC) DESIGN CENTER

N. Morgan, Chicago . IL

On its website, Green Home Chicago announces that the company has a dual purpose: "We sell unique and uncommonly beautiful eco-chic interior design products for commercial and residential sites. At the same time we are dedicated to the health of the planet, its inhabitants and our economy." Karen Kalmek, a co-owner and the designer of the GHC Design Center explains further, "Green is exploding as a major social, political and economic issue worldwide. Therefore, we practice a new form of entrepreneurial cultivation and collaboration. Our design center is one of a growing number of 'greenhouses' for this rapidly growing business sector."

If you want reclaimed timber, low VOC paints or adhesives or any other eco-friendly

products for home or commercial installation, you are likely to find it in the warm, woody, atmospheric, reclaimed/rehabbed space. In addition to cabinetry, flooring, counter tops, wall coverings, window treatments and furniture, GHC also offers products from local crafts persons, manufacturers and artists. "We support the local green movement creating jobs and reducing pollution," Kalmek says.

Located in what was formerly a loft space, the ancient oak floors were resanded and refinished with a water-based stain. Several walls were razed to open up the space, but the doors that formerly connected the various rooms were reused in other areas of the shop. The original brick walls and the old timber joists of the ceiling and supporting columns

are exposed and add to the look of the furniture and furnishings set out on the floor. In keeping with the "green" theme, green Green Planet paint was used on the walls, and all the cabinetry was made of either local or FSC-approved woods. Water-based or natural wax finishes were applied and the core material are urea-free formaldehydes—and non-toxic adhesives were utilized. Much of the furniture was made by local artisans because "supporting local community is a priority of our business." Kelmak continues, "As we support community building and poverty alleviation, several of our rugs are from ARZU—a not-for-profit organization that brings in rugs from Afghanistan." These rugs are hand-woven, colored with natural dyes and woven by women who then have an income for food and health uses. The live green plants that add to the residential, lived-in feeling of the space add natural beauty while improving the indoor air quality.

The GHC Design Center is proof of what Kelmak and her partner, Bill Homer, believe, "Green can be chic, inviting and uncommonly beautiful" and this showroom/shop is what greening is all about.

Design / Sarah Ellsworth, LEED AP of McBride Kelly & Bauer; Karen Kalmek, GHC Design Center
Owners / Karen Kalmek & Bill Homer
Photography / Katrina Wittkamp

"Lion Brand is a 130-year-old, family-owned company. This is the company's first retail venture. Our challenge was to create a new design concept that would promote both yarn and the activities of knitting and crocheting. It had to be modern and functional but also comfortable and welcoming. The studio reflects that balance with clean design, innovative displays, state-of-the-art lighting and environmentally friendly materials—and it's a great place for people to knit in a community setting. I believe this studio is the first of its kind." That was the statement made by David Gauld, the NYC-based architect/designer, who created this Lion Brand Yarn Studio on W. 15th St., just off of the rejuvenated Union Square in NY.

The almost all-glass shop front allows the daylight to flood in and offers passersby the first view of the old rough brick back wall and the earth-colored bamboo flooring. The 1700 sq. ft. space occupies what was once offices in this 1920 loft building. A curved blue wall, up front, draws shoppers into a celebration of color and craft. The "breaks" in the undulating waves create zones for different activities. In one of these breaks—near the front of the shop—is a sampling area filled with cactus-like fixtures made of plumbing pipes and fittings. Resting on the provided spikes are

cones of yarn from which shoppers are welcome to cut off swatches for matching or testing. A unique display, on the opposite wall, offers visitors the widest variety of Lion Brand colors in one place. The ice-like, diagonal cubbies that hold the yarns are constructed of translucent polycarbonate panels and backlit and illuminated from above as well. Mostly fluorescent lamps have been used for general illumination, along with some metal halide lamps. A few sparingly placed low-voltage halogen lamps were added, but since energy efficiency and conservation was a prime consideration, the reduced heat emission from the lamps cuts down on the air-conditioning output.

A map-like grid on the ceiling and the bamboo flooring anchor and orient the waves and diagonal shapes. References to nature are reinforced throughout by the use of numerous recycled and renewable materials. The resin counters and ceramic tile floors are made from recycled glass, and the cabinets are fashioned from boards made of reclaimed sorghum plant stalks bonded to poplar (a rapidly renewable wood) with a formaldehyde-free

bonding agent. Only water-based paints were used and the ceiling tiles are free of formaldehyde-based resins. Even the bamboo floor has a water-based, solvent-free finish.

With a Learning Bar where the staff offers assistance on knitting and crocheting projects, as well as demonstrations on various yarn crafting techniques, there is access to free patterns via the computers available near the cash desk. "This is not just a store but a center of inspiration, education and service for those who knit or crochet," said David Blumenthal, president of Lion Brand Yarns.

"While certain raw materials refer to the past industrial nature of the building and the neighborhood, other elements are used to create a sense of comfort and domesticity associated with the art and craft of knitting and crocheting, contemporized for our time," said Gauld.

Design / David Gauld Architect, NYC
Client Team / Karen Tanaka, Creative Director
Photography / Interiors: Paul Johnson, Stamford, CT; Façade: David Gauld

The major challenge for the design team at tvsdesign of Atlanta was to renovate a dilapidated interior space in an historical building constructed in 1910 to a contemporary furniture showroom. The project needed to incorporate sustainable design practices on a tight construction budget. The client, Kimball Office Furniture, wanted a showroom that would articulate their strong presence in wood furniture design and reflect the company's culture, while showcasing its manufacturing capabilities.

For the architects/designers at tvsdesign, this project meant dealing with uneven floors and wall surfaces, peeling paint, close column spacing, and non-code compliant toilets. It did not help that they were required to use the original steam-heating system, the irregular radiator sizes and that the space was not air conditioned. In addition, the designers were limited in what they could do with regard to floor penetration for the electrical and plumbing lines.

In solving the problems, significant floor leveling was accomplished and a suspended ceiling was incorporated in the areas where the furniture vignettes would be presented. This not only concealed the poor condition of the original ceiling but allowed a clearance for the new air-conditioning ductwork, while providing an office-like feel—replicating how visitors might experience furniture

in their own spaces. Rather than ignore the close spacing of the columns, the designers extended the size of the column lengths, providing separation of the furniture set-ups or vignettes, and also allowing space for the manufacturer's graphics. A code-compliant, flat-tape under-carpet system for electrical, telephone and data lines was utilized to avoid floor penetration while enabling the flexible placement of furniture clusters.

Visitors are greeted by "expressive" sycamore wood panels as they enter the third floor space, and the rhythm of the sycamore panels leads one to a dynamic floating wall made of reconstituted ebony veneer with oversized letter cutouts of the brand name. Visitors are

visually conducted through the showroom by a longitudinal ceiling plane that runs the length of the showroom. Recessed ceiling planes reflect the grid lines of the close column placement and the columns are articulated with floating panels covered with formaldehyde-free, 100% recovered and recycled fiber. These panels continue the "rhythm" established at the entrance with the sycamore paneling. This also serves as a blank canvas for graphic displays. Throughout, the designers maintained a sophisticated palette of chocolate brown and white accented with punches of poppy red.

Kimball's GreenGuard furniture and products are used throughout, and the showroom materials contain high recycled content, or

make use of rapidly renewable sources, low-emitting materials and supplies available locally or regionally. More than 90% of the equipment and appliances are Energy Star-rated, and more than 75% of construction waste was diverted from landfills. Sub-metering of systems was provided, which promotes responsible energy and water use/ conservation, and low-flow plumbing fixtures were used in the new toilets.

Steve Clem, a principal and designer at tvsdesign, said, "By addressing the existing condition challenges head on, the design team provided solutions that exceeded the expectations of the client and wows visitors to their space." It also earned this Kimball Showroom LEED CI Silver certification.

Architecture & Design / tvsdesign, Atlanta, GA—Steve Clem, AIA, ASID, IIDA; Ingrida Martinkus, LEED AP
Lighting Design / Quentin Thomas Assoc., Douglaston, NY
Photography / Brian Gassel, tvsdesign

The same guiding principles introduced over half a century ago by Florence Knoll—updated and executed in green/sustainable materials and illuminated with energy efficient lighting—now serves for the basic design of the Knoll showrooms, including this one in Chicago's Merchandise Mart. As designed by the Knoll Design Group, in NY, it ensures that all Knoll showrooms maintain a constant image that is in keeping with the company's history.

In this showroom that features Knoll Furniture, Knoll Textiles and Knoll office systems, architectural panels establish dominant verticals and horizontals, products relate to each other in a way that facilitates a logical circulation and understanding of the show-room, and products are grouped according to what they do rather than what they are. In addition, like the Miami showroom, this one is also LEED certified as a place that is environmentally responsible and a healthy place to live and work. To attain that certification, the paints and adhesives that were used are low VOC, the Knoll Textile wall coverings and the carpet backings have high recycled contents, FSC-certified woods are used at the Knoll workstations, building materials are recycled and GreenGuard Indoor Air Quality furnishings and textiles are used.

Through the wide-glazed opening off the elevator, the showroom is on display with an assortment of Knoll desk chairs featured and there is also the blaze of red glow from the

illuminated wall with photo images of office workers in relaxing office chairs. Beyond is the neutral-colored showroom space—off-white polished concrete floors, white walls and ceilings, and an occasional flash of the signature Knoll red. The Knoll Textiles and leathers, artfully draped, add brilliant touches of color and a casual feeling to the showroom, where the furniture and furnishings are arranged in livable vignettes.

Previously, the Knoll employees' offices were one floor below and connected to the showroom by an internal stairway. With the new enlarged space—all on one level—a new challenge was offered. Karen Stone, director of design at Knoll Inc., said, "We found this an excellent opportunity to redesign. Our goal became finding a way to best demonstrate to our clients our best practices in promoting sustainable design. We relocated our staff office and work areas along the window

wall. This was an effort to afford employees best access to daylight. All of the products specified for staff and work areas are FSC and GreenGuard approved, manufactured regionally with recycled content. Window treatments were specified to allow flexibility by the users—we also specified controllability of the lighting system—which utilizes optimized energy performance fluorescent fixtures."

The Knoll showroom is a living example of Show & Tell; it proves that greening/ sustainability can be beautifully integrated into the work-space/market place.

Design : Knoll Design Group, New York—Karen Stone, Director of Design
LEED Consultant : Envision Design, Washington, DC—Kendall P. Wilson ,AIA, IIDA, LEED AP
Photography : Courtesy of Knoll, Inc.

Located in downtown Atlanta is the new 7000 sq.ft. showroom/office of the Interface company; a premier floor covering manufacturer which also happens to be a leading advocate of sustainable design initiatives. The tvsdesign firm, also of Atlanta, was called upon to create a showroom that was convenient to the client's customers, allows for exceptional flexibility in display and mock-ups of the multiple products, tells the client's image story, provides working space for staff, supports urban redevelopment and offers an effective entertainment environment for the company-sponsored special events. All of this was to be accomplished while being consistent to Interface's leadership in sustainable design. The project was designed and produced under the guidelines of the LEED CI pilot program and eventually was LEED's first platinum (the highest level) certified project in the U.S.

The showroom, which serves both wholesale and retail customers, resembles an urban loft and features exposed concrete floors combined with areas of bamboo flooring, and 12 ft. diameter lampshades serving to highlight specific areas in the space. Since the space is multi-purpose, it can be entirely open for special events or, by lowering the shades between the galleries, divided into exclusive retail residential zones. There is also a museum-like quality to the overall design with its neutral color palette that lets the flooring products on view to step forward and be seen. Easily changed, billboard-size graphics are used to affect areas of color and definition, and they incorporate product promotion and brand identity.

According to Steve Clem, principal of tvsdesign, "The Interface showroom represents the ultimate synergy between high-quality design, sustainability and human well-being. Occupants of the space are treated with superior indoor

air quality with low or no VOC's in the paints, adhesives, carpet, composite wood materials and furniture, zero use of CFCs (chlorofluorocarbons) in the HVAC&R equipment and extensive monitoring of the thermal comfort level."

The large, expansive space is also opened to the outdoors with large street front windows. The windows help maximize daylight and views from the inside, but also welcome the passerby into the store by presenting a welcoming, high-end facility.

To achieve the LEED rating, recycled materials were used, as well as many materials from the local region. The beech wood used on the millwork and the Bamtex (bamboo wood) flooring are both rapidly renewable materials. Construction and consumer waste was recycled and the contractor was able to reduce construction waste by 90% over conventional means. The materials used, as in Clem's quote above, were all on LEED's high-preference list. The daylight, also previously mentioned, helps to conserve energy as does the highly energy-efficient equipment, the appliances and the lighting and light controls.

The attractive showroom design not only pleases aesthetically, but is successful in effectively showcasing Interface's product lines. It also provides a safe, sustainable area where the well-being of the shoppers, the staff and the community as a whole are taken into consideration.

Design / tvsdesign, Atlanta, GA—Steve Clem, Principal
Photography / Brian Gassel, tvsdesign

The Merchandise Mart in Chicago serves as a major furniture designer showroom center and Mohawk Carpets, which encompasses four separate brand names, took over 9656 sq.ft. of the third floor of the massive building. The area consists of a rectangular space to the north of the main corridor and a triangular-shaped space to the south of the main artery. Envision Design of Washington, DC, transformed the larger rectangular space into a showroom in which the four brands of carpet are on display. The triangular area serves as a special display gallery, as well as for support functions such as offices, work stations and conference rooms. According to Kendall Wilson of Envision Design, "In an industry prone to trendy designs, the intent of this carpet showroom is to be minimal and timeless. It was felt that the showroom design should be restrained and not overwhelm the product." Also, the commission included the need to reinforce the Mohawk Group's commitment to sustainability, which the designers satisfactorily achieved. This showroom received LEED CI Gold-level certification.

The main showroom required openness and visibility to the entire space from any point within the display area. Glass walls and doors line the public corridor between the two spaces and they maximize views into the showrooms. Attracting attention, as well, is the floating rear-projection screen over and behind the reception desk. The video loop reinforces product brand imagery. The main showroom has been designed with flexibility foremost, and the neutral gray carpet becomes an ideal background for the newest carpet products. There is a circular traffic path around the centrally located sales area and the spaces between the millwork allow guests to pass through to the different locations. The many sample carpets are suspended on sliding display panels contained within pockets in the perimeter walls, while large display tables rest atop sample storage cabinets in the central sales zone.

In addition to the daylight that streams in, the uniform fluorescent lighting system throughout the showroom and the highly efficient T5 linear pendant fixtures provide even lighting similar to modern office conditions. Daylight sensory controls, occupancy sensors and dimmers control the lighting in the private offices, conference rooms and support offices. Energy Star-rated equipment adds to the energy-saving conservation included in this project.

In achieving Gold certification, the project scored high in renewable energy (100%), construction waste recycled (99%), and 84% of the wood used in the furniture, fixtures and construction is FSC (Forest Stewardship Council) certified. 40% of the furniture was salvaged and reused from the previous showroom, while all the new office furniture is GreenGuard certified. As another energy-saving element, almost 69% of the products and furniture in the construction were produced within a 500-mile radius of the Merchandise Mart and the building itself is LEED EB-certified.

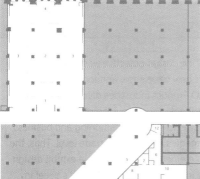

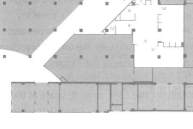

Design / Envision Design, Washington, DC—
Kendall P. Wilson, FAIA, FIIDA, LEED AP, Design
Principal/ Principal in charge; Robert P. Moylan,
IIDA Assoc, AIA, LEED AP; Ashley Compton, LEED
AP, IIDA Assoc.
Photography / Eric Laignel, NYC

The design objective was to design a new trade show unit for Timberland's PRO Product Industries division that would highlight the various product lines and embody PRO's brand positioning and business strategies aimed at the trade level. Thus, the key elements of this reusable exhibit design are in keeping with Timberland's belief in the importance of environmental values and sustainability, along with the unique branding and iconic attributes of the Timberland brand.

The modular design that was created originally for the 40 ft. by 40 ft. space at the World Shoe Association's show in Las Vegas is focused on bringing footwear to the market. Timberland PRO celebrates the everyday heroes that are its customers—the professional working consumers who require slip-proof, work and heavy-duty footwear. Inside, the display systems and job clipboards played up these "hero" stories and product lines. The signature PRO orange color appears predominantly on the skeletal framework of the exhibit

and the superstructure carries the name and logo. Orange also appears on the reclaimed construction fencing and the warehouse-style racking elements inside. The structure was designed and assembled with the look and texture of scaffolding found around a construction site. The Unistrut structural channels and fillings also add an industrial feel to the space, as do the roll-up galvanized receiving doors that serve as flexible dividers that open or close to create intimate conferencing spaces inside. They also assist in the transportation process between show appointments in the style of contractor's job box graphics. The Timberland PRO logo on the ribbed panels serves to further brand the exhibit space. The translucent wall panels are constructed of a material similar to postal carrying boxes. The flooring of recycled rubber plates further underscores the company's position on greening. Energy Star bulbs were used to illuminate the exhibit and they were set into industrial magnet mounts.

Found, repurposed, recycled and re-processed elements and materials are used extensively in the design and construction of the exhibit. The outside of the booth features a three-dimensional "nutrition label"—a signature element that is part of the outdoor performance packaging that here highlights the various green and sustainable materials used. It becomes an environmental "scorecard" for Timberland's full transparency and accountability. Some of these materials include the biodegradable flooring material (Marmoleum); Valchromat—a wood-like board produced from pine tree forest scraps and made without the use of formaldehyde and stained with organic dyes; Flakeboard—made from strands of trembling Aspen—a self-regenerating hardwood; cork; hemp and Echo Eliminator—a recyclable sound absorbing material. The booth is modular in concept and thus can be used in many different configurations. It can be reinvented without additional expenditure of materials and it is assumed that at the end of its five-year lifetime it will be 82% recyclable.

Ken Nisch, AIA and chairman of JGA, the retail design firm that created the exhibit, said, "Timberland has a focus on being green both 'coming and going,' with the overall booth achieving an 83% rating in eco-consciousness through its use of recycled, reused and reusable products. Eco-friendliness involves common sense, utility and finding the right tool for the right purpose, with a long view towards stewardship and sensible sustainability."

Design / JGA Inc., Southfield, MI—Ken Nisch, Chairman;
Gordon Eason, Creative Director
Client Team / Bevan Bloemendaal, Sr. Director, Global
Creative Services; Jean Wood, Fixturing Manager; Stephen
King, Sr. Manager of Corporate Events; Amy Tauchert, Sr.
Environments Manager; Linda Staniels, Project Manager,
Corporate Events; John Caley, Sr. Designer; Janice Cutler,
Designer
Fabrication / Concepts 360 Exhibits, Doylestown, PA
Photography / Mark Steele Photography, Columbus

As part of a global rebranding expansion for RED Protection, Burton Snowboards' helmet protection division, the environment for the S.I.A. Snowsport Trade Show in Las Vegas was an expansion of the company's "Ride Forever!" campaign created by Soldier Design. Red Protection called upon Bobby Riley and the Soldier Design team to create the exhibit booth and they worked specifically with Green Space on the booth because of their expertise on exhibits and environments and their intense focus on eco-friendly methods of completion. Sustainable materials and techniques were used in the finished product as shown here.

The central focus of the space is the re-used overseas shipping container that was reconditioned and repainted the signature RED color with low VOC paints. The container eliminated the need to construct a structure and the spacious interior serves as a container for all the fixtures and displayers when the exhibit is dismatled and shipped to its next location. This reduces waste. Riley, of Soldier Design, said,"RED, as a protection brand, has not lost focus on their #1 intent: to protect. The use of the cargo container, beyond smart sustainable reasons, represents protection—the icon of the space."

The logs that add texture to the ambiance are Pacific Albus, a poplar species, and the first logs harvested from the Collins Mill, a new, fully certified FCS-certified logging mill in Boardman, OR. In nine years, the Albus reaches its 40-ft. harvestable height. FSC-certified plywood was used for the counter, display boxes and mannequin platform and they were finished with low VOC paint. Tiles of recycled rubber tires covered the floor.

"Representing the brand and representing Spoldier Design's campaign intents, Green Space's use of the eco-friendly materials, design and building materials pulled the entire project together," said Riley. Rob Roth, president of Green Space added, "I appreciate the concise nature of the design intent and the flexibility to meet the objectives. It made it very easy to reach value-engineered situations that kept the design intact. Soldier's willingness to consider and incorporate environmentally sustainable options was music to our ears. It is the primary objective of our company."

The exhibit is scheduled for future re-use—as is.

Design / Soldier Design, Cambridge, MA & Green Space, Portland, OR—Bobby Riley, Creative Director & CEO of Soldier Design; Rob Roth, President of Green Design
Photography / Guy Lewis Photography

The Westfield Group, with 119 shopping centers worldwide, has just made the mall shopping experience not only richer and more eco-friendly, but educational as well. And—fun! Working closely with the L.A.-based designers of Rios Clementi Hale Studios, they have produced, according to Julie Smith-Clementi, IDSA, a partner in the design firm, "an experience made cohesive by decorative motifs and information about natural ecosystems, such as rainforests, oceans and mountains." One such installation appears in the Westfield Culver City Mall in Los Angeles.

"The goal was to create a program of amenities that would engage both kids and adults, and make the Westfield shopping center their destination for fun, food, education and shopping, while also making it easier for parents to navigate the mall," says Smith-Clementi. "As a bonus, the themes also promote eco-consciousness and healthy living to everyone who experiences it." Each theme, in this instance the rainforest, is produced in vivid colors, a variety of textures, with evocative sounds and elements that stimulate the senses. And—whenever possible—with natural and eco-friendly materials.

Signature motifs from the rainforest, like butterflies, flowers, exotic foliage, insects, monkeys and frogs, appear in bright and simple shapes and they are used to highlight the various areas in the mall, or as Smith-Clementi

puts it—"The graphic icons are akin to 'bread-crumbs' directing families through the mall," starting at the garage and into the center. These icons appear on columns in the dining area adjacent to the play space that is now the major attraction and draw in the central atrium. Giant butterfly mobiles soar overhead marking the location. These multi-colored, water-jet-cut aluminum shapes highlight the space.

The cutout of a barefoot monkey welcomes children—no taller than he is—to this focal zone. The interdependence of life is the focus of the play space, which features a leaf slide, flower seats and frog-shaped stools. There are cubby holes provided in the surrounding low walls where the children can store their shoes

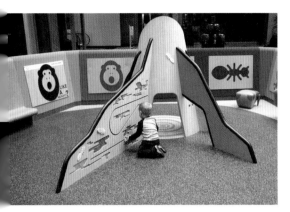

and things, as well as seating for parents. Here they can sit, relax and watch the children absorbing an eco-system education. The elements that make up this play are modular in design so that the concept can be adjusted to suit other spaces in other Westfield malls. The walls are organic, irregularly shaped and create a variety of zones within the enclosure.

The theme is also carried over into the family lounges, where parents with toddlers or infants can rest and rejuvenate in "natural" settings: colorful walls covered with rainforest murals and coordinated rugs on the floor. In addition to video programs for the little ones, there are private nursing rooms, changing rooms and toilets. In keeping with the environmental theme, wherever possible natural and eco-friendly materials were used in this project, including natural linoleum, renewable woods, and recycled rubber, carpets and plastics. As an example, the children's chairs in the dining area are made of 100% recycled, high-density polyethylene plastics.

Summing it up, Smith-Clkementi says, "All elements are consistent with story-telling and create shared moments of learning (about eco-sysrems and ecology) that are fun." That learning takes place in an eco-friendly produced space.

Design / Rios Clementi Hale Studios, Los Angeles
Photography / Jim Simmons

Ways for going green in the springtime, while still being fashionable, were provided in the New Renaissance windows at the Bay in Toronto. Here the message—in bold, green letters—informed shoppers of what they could do to go green: "Walk to Work," "Turn Off the Lights," "Reduce Packaging," "Reuse Your Bags" and "Think Green." In smaller letters, the design team offered numerous other ways the viewer could go green. The windows showed semi-abstract white mannequins in new spring outfits in a variety of clever ways, using—actually, reusing—props, decoratives and pieces that had been used before, but used in a new way to tell a vital story.

"Walk to Work" offered crossed legs shod in the season's newest shoes. For "Turn Off the Lights," naked abstract mannequins were barely visible through the translucent panels of the screens that stretched across the window with sleepwear and loungewear tossed over the screens, or falling to the floor.

Cardboard cartons were recycled along with the plastic peanuts used for packing to set the stage for "Reduce Packaging," while fur coats were casually draped over hot-pink-painted coat racks. Glove hands suspended on rods hanging from the ceiling held an array of colorful handbags that coordinated with the clothes on the dress forms, rising up from the floor in the "Reuse Your Bags" presentation. Green bulbs glowed from atop the mannequins' heads in "Think Green," along with pink-painted arms extending from the rear wall, offering a selection of fashion accessories.

These displays were enhanced by a follow-through inside the store, where similar graphics and green statements appeared in focal areas on every floor.

Client / the Bay, Toronto—Ana Fernandes, Creative Design Director; Denis Frenette, Director of ISM Field and Visual Presentation
Photography / James Dioron

Everything old—and used—is new again, and if the viewer seeing these exciting Christmas windows looks very closely, the observer will find much he or she has seen before in another "life"—another form—another display.

The theme for Harvey Nichols' holiday windows was "Rejoice and Recycle," a call to reuse and repurpose, while making do with some of the things you have while, adding some things that are new and in fashion. These were windows one did not casually stroll by. They beckoned to the shopper on the

street—drew them closer—and then invited them to recognize all the items that have so cleverly been recycled into the battery of windows with the theme running from one into the next. Many of the recycled items are quite small and the difference is in the details, which are numerous here. Old Christmas cards, reused and refashioned wrapping papers, stored glass ornaments brought out to add luster and shine one more time, strings of lights that have graced many previous holiday windows all come together with a new purpose. Like Marley's ghost in *A Christmas Carol*, it is a visit to Christmases past—to Christmas present—and a look ahead to Christmases yet to be—if we recycle.

Client / Harvey Nichols, Knightsbridge, London, UK—Janet Wardley, VM Controller; Laura O'Connor, Company Window Display Manager
Photography / Melvyn Vincent

EARTH DAY @ MACY'S

Macy's flagship, Herald Square, New York

Recycling was the message delivered by Paul Olszewski, director of windows, and his design/display team in the Macy's flagship store on Herald Square in NYC. In the all-white surround of the window, lumps, piles, bound masses of recycled or ready for recycling volumes filled the central space of each window. White, semi-abstract mannequins in contemporary outfits appeared and interacted with these unsightly newpapers, cartons, and plastic and aluminum containers.

Green was the message and on the front glass—in green letters—an education was offered in why and how recycling is a valuable asset in helping the earth back to health.

WM's landfills provide more than 10,000 acre
33 are certified by the Wildlife Habitat Counci

ecycling more than 3.5 million tons of newspaper, office paper and cardboard,
million trees were saved.

By recycling more than 257,000 tons of pla
enough energy was saved to power almos

cs,
30,000 houses for one year.

In the simple, succinct and easy-to-read sentences, viewers on the street were offered statistics about how recycling can be used to create necessary energy and also save on energy costs.

The "WM" logo, for "Waste Management," and the "Think Green" imprint appeared on the front glass as well—as a seal of approval, but also as a credit line for providing the recycled/recyclable waste material that served as the main display props. WM also provided many of the facts that appeared on the window. The imaginative headdresses on the mannequins tied in with the recyclable materials and they were created by the display personnel.

Client / Macy's Herald Square, NYC—Paul Olszewski, Director of Windows
Photography / Courtesy of Macy's Herald Square, NYC

Sony Style used its imposing windows on fashionable Madison Ave. in NYC to reiterate its commitment to greening and sustainability. Christine Belich, Sony Style's vp of visual explained, "Sony is commited to being an innovative environmental corporate citizen by creating the ultimate closed-loop product life cycle. Our company is developing innovative and effective methods of using recycled materials; innovative production processes; building energy-efficient products; and making it easier to recycle Sony products. All of this reaffirms Sony's commitment to sustainability."

The theme for these windows was "Eco-Innovations," and the major window told the whole story: "Designing Tomorrow—Rethink—Renew—Reduce." The window set-ups juxtaposed the intricacies of the linear networks of digital mechanisms with elements of

nature such as trees, grass, and earth. Green was the dominant color. The copy, in each display, succinctly explained how the Sony products on view worked with nature rather than against it. The design team incorporated large-format graphics, vinyl graphics, piles of earth and moss-covered mounds as well as gardening tools—"all to achieve a multi-layered feel. We started with the assets of the Sony.com/green website and embellished from there," said Belich. Though the designers used mostly traditional materials, many of them are reusable and will be repurposed in future displays. Other materials that were used had already appeared in previous Sony displays and had been revived for this new exposure.

The items that were featured are some of Sony's top green products, such as the VAIO

Building a sustainable
future through innovation.

Thinner, lighter VAIO
require less ener

Eco-Innovations
Innovative green approaches for designing tomorrow.

Eco-Innovations
Innovative green approaches for designing tomorrow.

Experience energy-saving
entertainment with the new
BRAVIA® VE5 HDTV.

Eco-Innovations

Innovative green approaches for designing tomorrow.

Rethink
Renew
Reduce

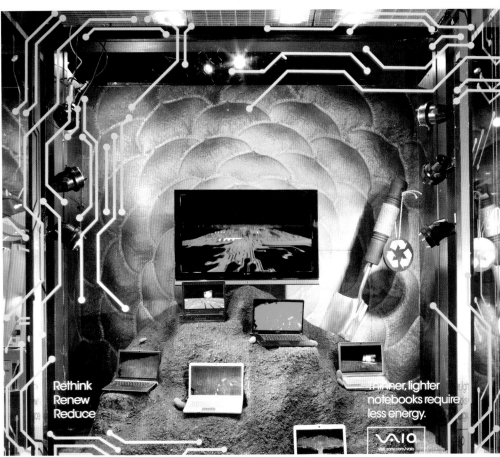

Rethink
Renew
Reduce

thinner, lighter
notebooks require
less energy.

VAIO
visit: sony.com/vaio

P Lifetime PC, Readers Touch and Pocket Editions, Digital Photo Frame and the new eco-friendly BRAVIA VE5 series televisions. The finishing touch—and another sensual accent—was the green-inspired fragrance Green Bamboo and that scent wafted out over the passersby who had stopped to admire the displays and study the products being featured.

When asked how a visual merchandiser/ display person contributes to the greening/ sustainability that is now becoming part of a company's brand image, Belich replied, "It's my job to help communicate Sony's programs and initiatives that encourage sustainability and promote best environmental practices to

consumers in a visually interesting way that helps them to understand that Sony Electronics is constantly looking for ways to have a positive impact on the planet. It's important to create high-impact windows that grab attention and make consumers stop to learn more. Our green initiative was a way to educate yet intrigue and offer positive attributes about the brand."

Design Team / Christine Belich, VP of Visual; Leigh Ann Tischler; Steven Stathakis
Design Contributors / Stewart Lucas; Mark Fugarino
Photography / Richard Cadan, New York

GLOSSARY

ALKEMI solid surfaces made of 35% post-consumer scrap metal.

ANSI/American National Standards Institute oversees the creation and promulgation of norms and guidelines to assure safety and health of consumers and the protection of the environment.

A.R.E./Association for Retail Environments An organization composed of store fixture manufacturers, retail design firms, the retail environment industry and visual merchandisers. Membership includes NASFM (National Association of Store Fixture Manufacturers) and NADI (National Association of Display Industries).

AVONITE recycled solid surfacing product that may resemble stone, marble, concrete, etc.

BAMTEX wood flooring material produced from bamboo. Eco-friendly and durable.

BIODEGRADABLE ability to decompose naturally in a relatively short period of time.

BIOFLEX a strong biodegradable polymer fabric.

CAESAR STONE solid surface material: includes 17% post-consumer recycled content.

CAGBC Canada Green Building Council

CAN/CSA Z809 Canadian National standard for managing sustainable forests.

CARBON FOOTPRINT the measurement of GHG (greenhouse gas) emissions into the atmosphere that is caused directly or indirectly by a product. The measurement of CO_2 emissions from a project on the climate.

CENTER FOR RESOURCE SOLUTIONS Audits and oversees the green power industry.

CFC Chlorofluorocarbons. The chlorine in CFC is one of the causes of the accelerated depletion of ozone in the Earth's atmosphere. *See* CO_2.

CFL Compact fluorescent lighting. Uses 1/4 to 1/3 less electricity than incandescent, lasts up to 10 times longer and produces 90% less heat.

CITIES Convention of International Trades Endangered Species

COMFORT E-PS low E glass = low emissive, energy efficient glass that meets Energy Star requirements in North America.

CO2 Carbon Dioxide. A gas produced from the use of fossil fuels that contributes to the greenhouse effect.

CPA/Composite Panel Association *See* EPP.

CRADLE-TO-CRADLE the use of a product from its creation through to its reuse in a recycled product.

CRI Carpet & Rug Institute

DAKOTA BURL a bio-based composite board made of waste sunflower husks that resembles traditional burled woods. A product of Environs Biocomposites.

DOE U.S. Department of Energy

DURAPRENE a wall covering material composed of latex-impregnated cellulose fibers made of 50% recycled fiber content.

ECHO ELIMINATOR a recyclable sound-absorbing material.

ECO-FRIENDLY products, materials and techniques that are kind to the environment. Often refers to sustainable and/or recycled materials and non-toxic emissions.

ECORESIN PANELS plastic panels made of 40% pre-consumer recycled resin with natural elements embedded—like bamboo or flower petals. A product of 3Form.

ECOX Recycled concrete that is 70% post-consumer and post-industrial.

EC+ E-Core plus boards. Lightweight and made of recycled materials and organic glues.

ENERGY STAR RATED Appliances that are energy efficient, according to Federal standards.

EPA Environmental Protection Agency

EPP The Composite Panel Association's certification of composite products made of recycled or recovered wood fibers. These panels have low formaldehyde emission.

EUROPLY non-urea formaldehyde plywood.

FLAKEBOARD boards made of strands from the trembling aspen tree.

FORMALDEHYDE a gas—CHO_2—that is used in resins. It is colorless and irritating to humans and animals. Urea formaldehyde, when used in resins, may produce a noxious gas. Phenol formaldehyde produces less of this gas.

FSC/Forest Stewardship Council an organization that promotes environmentally effective use of the world's forests.

FTC U.S. Federal Trade Commission

GEI/GreenGuard Environmental Institute organization that promotes improved health through better indoor air. Certifies products that are low emitting, like volatile organic compounds (VOC), assorted chemicals and carcinogens.

GEOTHERMAL WELLS wells dug deep into the earth that allow heat energy to be transported from the ground to the fluid that runs in the pipes that heat or cool the space. To cool the space heat is removed from the space and transferred to the loop fluid. As the fluid travels, the earth cools it and the heat is deposited in the ground.

GREENCHILL a certification program for food retail stores in recognition of their use of environmentally friendly commercial refrigeration systems. Refrigeration with zero ozone depleting potential.

GREEN GUARD (for indoor air) *See* GEI.

GREEN HOUSE EFFECT the effect of the buildup of CO2 and other gasses upon the Earth's lower atmosphere and surface.

GHG greenhouse gas

GREEN POWER PARTNERSHIP organization that encourages use of green power as part of best-practice environmental management.

GPS global positioning system

GREEN ROOF roofs and terraces planted with plants, bushes and trees.

GREEN SEAL organization that promotes products and services that are eco-friendly. Offers certification of products that are ecologically sound.

GREEN STONE a molded stone-like material composed of recycled materials and minerals.

HCFC Refrigeration system a coolant system based on hydrogen, chlorine, fluorine and carbon.

HFC Refrigeration system a coolant system based on hydro fluorocarbon (hydrogen/fluorine/carbon).

HID LAMPS high-intensity discharge lamps. Compact, high-efficiency lamps. See Metal Halide Lamp.

HVAC heating, ventilation and air conditioning

HVAC+R: heating, ventilation, air conditioning + refrigeration

ICC International Code Council. *See* SBTC.

KIREI BOARD a wood substitute used for millwork and furniture. Strong, lightweight and durable, it is made of reclaimed sorghum straw with no added formaldehyde adhesive.

LED/Light Emitting Diode not the traditional light bulb. According to GE, "LEDs are a solid-state device that do not require a filament to create light. Rather electricity passes through a chemical compound that is excited and generates heat." LEDs need to be placed on a circuit board that will allow electricity to pass through at a specific voltage and current. There are LED bulbs, strips, clusters, etc.

LEED Leadership in Energy and Environmental Design. *See* p. 10.

LEED-CI LEED Commercial Interiors certification

LOHAS Lifestyle of Health and Sustainability. *See* p. 80.

LOW VOLTAGE HALOGEN LAMPS smaller, brighter and last longer than incandescent lamps but gives off more heat and requires a transformer.

MARMOLEUM A biodegradable flooring or surfacing material made of natural ingredients such as linseed oil, cork, limestone and tree resins. Uses no VOC resins, is odor-free and emits no gasses into the atmosphere.

MDF/Medium density fiberboard wood fibers combined with wax and a resin binder—under heat and pressure—to form boards used in furniture and construction. Similar to plywood and denser than particle board.

METAL HALIDE LAMP part of the HID family of lamps. Has higher light output for its size and is energy efficient.

MRTAG Material & Resources Technical Advisory Board.

NLPIP/National Lighting Product Information Program. *See* PV LIGHTING

NPI National Power Initiative

PEFC/Programme for Endorsement of Forest Certification agreed upon by 37 pan-European nations in order to protect the forests of Europe. To document and improve sustainable forest management with regard to economic, ecological and social standards. *See* FSC.

PLYBOO formaldehyde-free and FSC-certified bamboo plywood and flooring manufactured by Smith & Fong Co.

PRSM/Professional Retail Store Management organization that develops tools, resources and education on sustainability for retail store operations and maintenance.

PV LIGHTING photovoltaic lighting. The light source is powered by batteries that are recharged by direct current (DC) electricity that is produced by the photovoltaic array, which gets its power from the sun. A photovoltaic collection system harvests power from the sun to create clean energy. Produced by National Lighting Product Information Program (NLPIP).

REC Renewable Energy Certificates

RECS INTERNATIONAL association of market players trading renewable energy certificates throughout Europe.

RENEWABLE ENERGY energy provided from a source which is not depletable but is regenerative, such as solar energy, wind power or hydropower.

SBTC/Sustainable Building Technology Committee created the International Green Construction Code. Focuses on design and performance of new and existing commercial buildings. Initiated by ICC to reduce energy usage and carbon footprint of commercial buildings.

SCS/Scientific Certification System certifies environmental claims for manufactured materials or products.

SEER/Seasonal Energy Efficiency Ratio the higher the SEER rating, the better and more efficient the air conditioning system.

SENSORS instruments that are sensitive to light, heat or movement and can save energy by turning off lights when no one is in the room or turn up heat when needed—or turn off the heat when room needs cooling down. Daylighting control sensors are used to monitor the daylight conditions in an area.

SKY BLEND a particle board developed by Rosenburg Forest Products that is made of 100% pre-consumer recycled wood fiber with no urea formaldehyde added. Low emission standards and made of sustainable raw materials.

SPINNEYBECK a leather fabric. A by-product of the meat industry. Tanning, dyeing and finishing meet or exceed all environmental requirement. No VOC and 100% post-consumer recyclable. GreenGuard certified.

SUSTAINABILITY "The use of a renewable system that can be retained in its essential characteristics and that can be renewed in as natural way" (Umdasch Shop Systems). Being capable of meeting our needs without affecting the needs of seven future generations.

3DEGREES Delivers customized global climate change solutions to U.S. business institutions.

USGBC U.S. Green Building Council., sponsor of LEED Certification.

VALCHROMAT a wood-like board produced from pine forest scraps that is formaldehyde free.

VCT Vinyl Composition Tile

VOC/Volatile Organic Compound compounds that appear in the gas chromatogram between and including N-hexane and N-hexadecane. Usually emits a noxious odor.

LEED-NC

LEED-NC Version 2.2 Registered Project Checklist
<< enter project name >>
<< enter city, state, other details >>

Yes	?	No				Points
8	**2**	**4**	**Sustainable Sites**			**14** Points
Y			Prereq 1	**Construction Activity Pollution Prevention**		Required
Y			Credit 1	**Site Selection**		1
Y			Credit 2	**Development Density & Community Connectivity**		1
		N	Credit 3	**Brownfield Redevelopment**		1
Y			Credit 4.1	**Alternative Transportation**, Public Transportation Access		1
Y			Credit 4.2	**Alternative Transportation**, Bicycle Storage & Changing Rooms		1
		N	Credit 4.3	**Alternative Transportation**, Low-Emitting and Fuel-Efficient Vehicles		1
Y			Credit 4.4	**Alternative Transportation**, Parking Capacity		1
	?		Credit 5.1	**Site Development,** Protect of Restore Habitat		1
Y			Credit 5.2	**Site Development,** Maximize Open Space		1
	?		Credit 6.1	**Stormwater Design,** Quantity Control		1
Y			Credit 6.2	**Stormwater Design,** Quality Control		1
		N	Credit 7.1	**Heat Island Effect,** Non-Roof		1
		N	Credit 7.2	**Heat Island Effect,** Roof		1
Y			Credit 8	**Light Pollution Reduction**		1

Yes	?	No				Points
2	**1**	**2**	**Water Efficiency**			**5** Points
Y			Credit 1.1	**Water Efficient Landscaping**, Reduce by 50%		1
		N	Credit 1.2	**Water Efficient Landscaping**, No Potable Use or No Irrigation		1
		N	Credit 2	**Innovative Wastewater Technologies**		1
Y			Credit 3.1	**Water Use Reduction**, 20% Reduction		1
	?		Credit 3.2	**Water Use Reduction**, 30% Reduction		1

Yes	?	No				Points
7	**2**	**2**	**Energy & Atmosphere**			**17** Points
Y			Prereq 1	**Fundamental Commissioning of the Building Energy Systems**		Required
Y			Prereq 2	**Minimum Energy Performance**		Required
Y			Prereq 3	**Fundamental Refrigerant Management**		Required
5			Credit 1	**Optimize Energy Performance**		1 to 10
	?		Credit 2	**On-Site Renewable Energy**		1 to 3
		N	Credit 3	**Enhanced Commissioning**		1
Y			Credit 4	**Enhanced Refrigerant Management**		1
		N	Credit 5	**Measurement & Verification**		1
Y			Credit 6	**Green Power**		1

Yes	?	No				
6		7	**Materials & Resources**			**13 Points**

Y			Prereq 1	**Storage & Collection of Recyclables**		Required
		N	Credit 1.1	**Building Reuse**, Maintain 75% of Existing Walls, Floors & Roof		1
		N	Credit 1.2	**Building Reuse**, Maintain 100% of Existing Walls, Floors & Roof		1
		N	Credit 1.3	**Building Reuse**, Maintain 50% of Interior Non-Structural Elements		1
Y			Credit 2.1	**Construction Waste Management**, Divert 50% from Disposal		1
		N	Credit 2.2	**Construction Waste Management**, Divert 75% from Disposal		1
		N	Credit 3.1	**Materials Reuse**, 5%		1
		N	Credit 3.2	**Materials Reuse**,10%		1
Y			Credit 4.1	**Recycled Content**, 10% (post-consumer + ½ pre-consumer)		1
Y			Credit 4.2	**Recycled Content**, 20% (post-consumer + ½ pre-consumer)		1
Y			Credit 5.1	**Regional Materials**, 10% Extracted, Processed & Manufactured Regiona		1
Y			Credit 5.2	**Regional Materials**, 20% Extracted, Processed & Manufactured Regiona		1
		N	Credit 6	**Rapidly Renewable Materials**		1
Y			Credit 7	**Certified Wood**		1

Yes	?	No				
11	2	2	**Indoor Environmental Quality**			**15 Points**

Y			Prereq 1	**Minimum IAQ Performance**		Required
Y			Prereq 2	**Environmental Tobacco Smoke** (ETS) **Control**		Required
Y			Credit 1	**Outdoor Air Delivery Monitoring**		1
Y			Credit 2	**Increased Ventilation**		1
Y			Credit 3.1	**Construction IAQ Management Plan**, During Construction		1
Y			Credit 3.2	**Construction IAQ Management Plan**, Before Occupancy		1
Y			Credit 4.1	**Low-Emitting Materials**, Adhesives & Sealants		1
Y			Credit 4.2	**Low-Emitting Materials**, Paints & Coatings		1
Y			Credit 4.3	**Low-Emitting Materials**, Carpet Systems		1
Y			Credit 4.4	**Low-Emitting Materials**, Composite Wood & Agrifiber Products		1
Y			Credit 5	**Indoor Chemical & Pollutant Source Control**		1
		N	Credit 6.1	**Controllability of Systems**, Lighting		1
		N	Credit 6.2	**Controllability of Systems**, Thermal Comfort		1
Y			Credit 7.1	**Thermal Comfort**, Design		1
Y			Credit 7.2	**Thermal Comfort**, Verification		1
	?		Credit 8.1	**Daylight & Views**, Daylight 75% of Spaces		1
	?		Credit 8.2	**Daylight & Views**, Views for 90% of Spaces		1

Yes	?	No				
3			**Innovation & Design Process**			**5 Points**

Y			Credit 1.1	**Innovation in Design**: Provide Specific Title		1
Y			Credit 1.2	**Innovation in Design**: Provide Specific Title		1
			Credit 1.3	**Innovation in Design**: Provide Specific Title		1
			Credit 1.4	**Innovation in Design**: Provide Specific Title		1
Y			Credit 2	**LEED® Accredited Professional**		1

Yes	?	No			
37	7		**Project Totals** (pre-certification estimates)		**69 Points**

Certified 26-32 points   **Silver** 33-38 points   **Gold** 39-51 points   **Platinum** 52-69 points

Index of Design Firms

For more information on visual merchandising and store design, subscribe to:

Experience Retail Now

**Books on visual merchandising and store design
available from ST Media Group International:**

Aesthetics of Merchandising Presentation
Budget Guide to Retail Store Planning & Design
Complete Guide to Effective Jewelry Store Display
Feng Shui for Retailers
Retail Renovation
Retail Store Planning & Design Manual
Stores and Retail Spaces
Visual Merchandising
Visual Merchandising and Store Design Workbook

**To subscribe, order books or request a complete catalog
of related books and magazines, please contact:**

MEDIA
GROUP
INTERNATIONAL

ST Media Group International Inc.
11262 Cornell Park Drive. | Cincinnati, Ohio 45242

p: 1.800.925.1110 or 513.421.2050
f: 513.421.5144 or 513.744.6999
e: books@stmediagroup.com
www.bookstore.stmediagroup.com (ST Books)
www.vmsd.com (*VMSD* Magazine)
www.irdconline.com (International Retail Design Conference)